Youth's Marriage Problems

OTHER BOOKS BY DR. MURRAY

Youth's Problem Number One
Youth's Courtship Problems

YOUTH'S
marriage
PROBLEMS

❦

ALFRED L.
MURRAY

Zondervan Publishing House
GRAND RAPIDS, MICHIGAN

Eight Forty-seven Ottawa Avenue
Grand Rapids, Michigan

Dedicated
to
my daughter, Marilyn A., and
my son, Alfred F.,
the source of much information
and inspiration

FOREWORD

During the three years in which I served with the United States Navy in World War II I came to see that unhappy marriages were one of the worst casualties of the war.

Crossing the Atlantic Ocean forty-four times with men going to and from battle, and then going to the Pacific after the fall of Germany, I came in contact with hundreds upon hundreds of men whose most pressing burden was the anxiety of broken homes. Men who had been faithful to their wives returned to discover that their mates had played the harlot, and women who waited prayerfully and patiently for the return of their husbands found that their reward for fidelity was desertion for divorce.

I saw the tragedy of hasty marriages, formed on short acquaintance, and read the letters written by brides of a few months who were seeking help in locating their husbands. I recall the case of a girl who rode for days on a bus to see her husband, from whom she had been receiving letters mailed at a base where I was stationed. Her husband had not been in that area for months, but was a few hours' ride from where she lived.

As Welfare Officer I read the letters of wives informing their husbands that they were ill, but that they were not to come home. Frequently special liberty revealed that the women were about to give birth to illegitimate children.

Men could endure the heat of battle if they were happy, but a disrupted marital life mowed them down like mortar fire.

Time after time I asked men and women, "Why did you marry this person?" Invariably the answer was: "I don't know." Statistics support the evidence that in America thousands upon thousands of young people are marrying without knowing why they take the solemn vows. The Marital Relations Institute of New York City submitted questionnaires to approximately 40,000 men and women in America's principal cities who were applying for marriage licenses. The first question was: "Why are you marrying?" Only 18,000 out of 40,000 answered the question. Only 9 percent of the 18,000 gave reasons for marrying, and approximately a fourth said that they were marrying to fulfill only one basic urge: "security." Less than 1 percent planned to rear a family. Why are people marrying? This question should be answered by every youth contemplating marriage. One must know why he wants to pledge his life to another "until death us do part."

Divorce and desertion threaten to destroy marriage. Divorce has tripled in forty-five years, and if it continues its present rate of increase, soon there will be one divorce for every marriage, thus making marriage meaningless. The "poor man's divorce" — separation without divorce — is still prevalent. Add to this the number of couples who are living together for convenience' sake but who have nothing in common. The institution of marriage, which is basic to America's social, spiritual and national life, is endangered. The future of marriage is uncertain because many people do not know why they marry.

The security of family life and happiness in marital relationship are guaranteed by a return to a sane attitude toward marriage. It is not a sport: it is a sacrament. It is not to be annulled by a judge but by The Judge. That religion is a guarantee of happy marital relations is not a pious platitude, but a statement supported by statistics.

Courses of study in marital relations are imperative, but they are not enough. To know about the duties and responsibilities in marriage is not enough unless one has the desire to "do justly . . . and to walk humbly with . . . God."

The security of family life is guaranteed by a return to the One who first united man and woman in marriage.

A Bible course is more important than a course in sexology. Proper technique in prayer is more essential than skillful sex technique. A wholesome attitude toward God is fundamental; a sane attitude toward sex is invaluable. The family counselor is desirable; the Wonderful Counselor is indispensable.

This book is an attempt to inform the mind and inspire the spirit of young people who want to make their married life beautiful and abiding. Only information and inspiration can help to preserve the sacrament of a divine institution — marriage.

Westerly, R. I.

ALFRED L. MURRAY

CONTENTS

WHY PEOPLE MARRY

CHAPTER 1

Why People Marry

ONE of the most significant and serious problems a young person faces is that of marriage. The choice of a mate may be made in a very short time, but the results of that decision may endure throughout life and make it a blessing or a curse. The happiness that comes from the choice of a right partner makes a peaceful home where two or more people live in joy and contentment and share responsibilities and pleasures. Children born in such an environment are heirs of that heritage which will enrich their lives as they grow into maturity.

The unwise choice of a companion in marriage is a tragedy. It leaves a train of sorrow and maladjustment that destroys one physically, socially, mentally and spiritually. Broken homes are the evil result of loosely-tied wedding bands. Many mentally and physically sick adults were healthy until they entered into an unwise marriage. One cannot live unhappily in the intimate confines of matrimony without breaking in mind or body or both.

Because marriage involves tremendous responsibility some people avoid it and cling to what is mistakenly called "single bliss." Others dash into matrimony without taking time to inquire what it is or why they should or should not marry. It is not uncommon to hear a married person say, "I do not know why I ever married." Many times I have heard military personnel who had been separated from their wives for some months say, "I don't know why I ever married her anyway." Wives wishing to be free from husbands in uniform have expressed their desire in these words: "Our marriage was a mistake." When asked why it was a mistake and who made it so, they invariably replied, "I guess neither of us knew what marriage was all about." Rarely did anyone blame himself.

The majority marry freely and of their own choice. There is no longer a stigma connected with a failure to conform. No penalties, except income tax, are imposed upon men who prefer to remain single, though this is a somewhat recent innovation. In ancient Sparta unmarried men of eligible age were penalized. Rome imposed a heavy fine upon her unmarried men of eligible age. Athens permitted only married men to aspire to public oratory. No such restrictions are now placed on bachelors. Unmarried men receive attention that is sometimes denied their married friends.

An American girl may remain single and not embarrass herself or her parents. She will be the object of neither pity nor scorn. Public opinion will not force her into marriage for the sake of being married. To get the daughters married is no longer the chief concern of the family. Most parents are more interested in their daughter's happiness than in "getting her a man." Changing family conditions have brought about this attitude. In other years, daughters placed a financial burden on their father, but now they are in a position to help him pay off the mortgage. Today girls hold lucrative positions, dress themselves well and possibly add to the family exchequer.

Forced marriages are no longer given wholesale community approval. Once a sure way for a girl to acquire a husband was for her to become pregnant to an unmarried man. Public opinion forced the man to marry the expectant mother. The time has come when the practice of insisting that a man marry a woman because he "got her into trouble" is on the decline. The child's interests demand a loving stepfather or foster father more than a disinterested male whose name the child may bear. There is, furthermore, a feeling that the problem may not be the man's sole responsibility. Each case is considered in the light of individual circumstances. Public opinion is willing that the girl who plays fast and loose with morals should pay the price for her misconduct. The parties involved in premarital sex relationships that result in the birth of an illegitimate child often do not consider the solution to be a forced marriage.

A soldier told a woman, who was going to have a child to him that he would pay for the baby but that he wanted nothing more to do with her. Newspapers recently carried the story of an unmarried girl who gave birth to a child whose father was a soldier. The mother told the young man that she did not want him nor the baby.

"Marriage is a social, spiritual, physical and legal institution. It is a cluster of customs and group habits, of attitudes, ideas and ideals; of sacred definitions and legal restrictions." "It is not to be entered into unadvisedly or lightly, but reverently, discreetly, advisedly, soberly and in the fear of God." Those who enter into it with study and forethought will not only enjoy its bliss but will have the well wishes and approval of society.

God saw that it was "not good that the man should be alone." Washington Irving observed that a married man falling into misfortune was "more apt to retrieve his situation in the world than a single one," as the latter was "apt to run to waste and self-neglect, to fall to ruins like some deserted mansion for want of an inhabitant." Voltaire declared that "marriage renders a man more virtuous and more wise." He contended that an unmarried man was "but half of a perfect being," and that a wife was required "to make things right." The United States census reveals that most Americans agree with the French philosopher. The census shows that 90 per cent of the persons who live to be fifty or older marry. There are more than a million marriages in the United States annually. A new height was reached in 1942 when a total of 1,800,000 marriages was recorded.

People marry because they want to do so of their own volition. They willingly assume the obligations and responsibilities of marriage because some innate power drives them to the altar. Why do they marry?

There are three basic urges in human life. These inherent needs are: the need for security; the need for significance; the need for love. All three needs express themselves in early childhood and, in a normal individual, increase in power

with the years. As one approaches marriageable age a combination of these basic needs is revealed in a wholesome
attitude toward members of the opposite sex. Thoughtful
people seek security, significance and love in marriage. A
combination of all three desires, or three expressions of
one paramount desire, should lead to a happy selection of
a mate. These three basic urges belong together and when
torn apart they lead to unhappy and unfortunate results in
wedlock.

Marriages are bound to fail when they are motivated by
other than a combination of these basic urges. Those who
wed for other purposes thwart their natural basic desires
which seek fulfillment in matrimony. These urges when not
satisfied seek a substitute which results in maladjustment
and disharmony in the union. People marry to satisfy these
innate desires, unless abnormal interests prompt the choice
of a mate. These abnormal desires may be an escape
mechanism, an inflated ego, rationalization or uncontrolled
sex desires.

A girl who marries to evade unfavorable home conditions,
to escape another suitor or to overcome loneliness is using
marriage as an escape mechanism.

The egocentric person marries to satisfy an inflated ego.
He selects someone who can give him material possessions,
such as an expensive car or a costly home, or who flatters
him into thinking he is "somebody." Any girl who can make
him feel important is his choice. An egocentric girl may
marry a man of whom she can boast to her friends, "He gave
me a big diamond and a fur coat." Such a marriage may
proceed smoothly until something occurs which alters the
foundation on which it was built. The expensive car may

wear out or the furs may deteriorate. Time may cause the flattery to cease, and then quarreling begins.

A girl was married in a distant state and came home by plane to visit her friends. Her diamonds were conspicuous and she was dressed in the latest fashion. Apparently she was happily married. One day her untactful sister paid her a surprise visit. The unwelcome visitor discovered that the girl worked in a store, that her husband was a poor laborer and that they lived in one room over a butcher shop. The husband had spent all his earnings on his wife and her extravagances had forced them into their present circumstances. As soon as her true financial condition was known to her family she became resentful, dissatisfied and soon deserted her husband.

The inflated ego demands satisfaction throughout marriage if the union is to be unbroken.

A more common abnormal cause of faulty marriages is rationalization. Rationalization may be part of an escape mechanism or an inflated ego, but it involves more. Rationalization is the ascribing of one's actions, behavior or decisions to acceptable motives. It offers excuses for every act. Lord Byron married Miss Milbank to obtain money to pay his debts, but he must have convinced himself as well as the lady that other than her money prompted his proposal.

Physical attractiveness has an important place in marriage. No one can be happy with a partner whose face is repulsive to him, but much more than physical beauty is required to make a married life beautiful.

Sir Walter Raleigh was wise in warning his son that if he was prompted to marry for beauty, "thou bindest thyself for life for that which will perhaps neither last nor please thee one year, and when thou hast it, it will be to thee of no price at all."

There are girls who marry men who have nothing to offer but a handsome appearance. Yet no girl would admit that she married a man because he had large brown eyes or curly hair. By the process of rationalization she justifies her marriage on more substantial bases.

A man may marry a girl who is pretty but in possession of an uncontrollable temper and lacks sound judgment. He attempts to explain away her weakness by attributing it to circumstances beyond her control.

The tragedy of rationalization in marriage is that for a time it closes one's eyes to the facts, but eventually they are opened to the true condition.

Admiration and sincerity, which are essential to a happy marriage, may be simulated by rationalization, but eventually the process ceases. "I knew all the time that there was nothing to the person I married," is a familiar remark. No one can long be a companion to someone he does not respect. Rationalization cannot serve as a permanent escape from reality.

Marriages prompted by unwarranted motives — a desire to conform to popular opinion, to please parents, to obtain a needed home, to express pity or gratitude to a suitor or to escape from a broken engagement — often find their excuse in rationalization.

A young lady married a man simply because he traveled and she liked to travel. Everything went well until his company made him manager of a local office. His wife became ill and required the attention of a psychiatrist. She was convinced that her husband possessed admirable qualities, but confessed that she had made herself believe she was in love with him, when what she truly loved was to travel. She married him because he could satisfy one desire. She finally took a position which enabled her to travel, and, although she remained married, lived apart from her husband most of the time.

People marry also to satisfy an awakened sexual desire. This is one reason why premarital sex relations are dangerous. They develop sex passion apart from a specific individual. Statistics show that those who "have to get married" are less likely to achieve marital happiness than married people who remain chaste. Sexual relationship is important in a happy marriage, but only when more than sex has brought the couple together. Those who are not forced into marriage but who have given themselves to premarital sexual relationships thus meet a disturbing factor in their marriage. They, likewise, undermine the possibilities of a happy relationship as man and wife. Anyone not convinced of this fact should read a scientific report on the subject.[1]

The normal urges, as has been stated, that lead people to marry are the desire for security, the desire for significance and the desire for love. These urges or forces seek in marriage an accepted pattern, by which a man and a woman may satisfactorily achieve certain specific ends and satisfy other basic and acquired desires or urges.

A desire for security is evident in the girl who marries for a home or for money, but this is on a low level. Desire has not reached the intellectual stage. When this urge is processed through the mind, it dissatisfies. The girl who gives thought to her marriage may want a home but she doesn't marry for the home alone. The desire for financial security

[1] Terman, L. M.. **Psychological Factors in Marital Happiness.**
[1] Hamilton, G. V., and MacGowan, Kenneth, **What Is Wrong With Marriage?**
[1] Exner, M. J., **The Sexual Side of Marriage.**

leads her to inquire into the mental and physical health of her prospective husband. She seeks to know something about his ability and willingness to work and to provide for herself and her children. She does not seek a man with a fortune but a man who can and will provide her with a security that will not leave her destitute and her children unfed.

Men marry because they, too, want a home, a companion or a partner. They look forward to having wives to share their burdens in time of adversity and trouble. A man marries a girl to guarantee that he will have a companion who will stand by him throughout life. There is an age-old longing, innate in everyone, for peace and security. The normal individual who satisfies this urge in marriage will be saved from unnatural fear, persistent indolence and possible infantile regression. No person who asks of marriage a normal sense of security should be accused of mercenary motives, but quite the contrary. He is planning intelligently for a home and a marriage that will last.

The desire for security helps to draw a man and his wife closer together. They plan for the interest and protection of each other and look forward to the future together. A common purpose unites and motivates them from the beginning of their marriage.

They establish goals, toward which they must strive, that will guarantee security to them in old age. They are led to think of their marriage as something permanent and rewarding. They marry for security and build upon a sound foundation.

But this urge will overlap. It will be supplemented by associated with or dominated by the urge for significance in marriage. As human beings we, according to Adler, live in the realm of meaning. "The individual must feel himself to be a being with meaning, for he cannot have human importance without it." The normal individual will strive to satisfy a feeling of being worth while. He must realize that this is necessary if his life is to be significant. It is the only way he can overcome his sense of inferiority, which is nurtured from infancy, and thus discover his importance to society. This urge for meaning or significance finds expression in marriage.

A man will marry a woman because she fires his ambition and makes him feel that he can do something vital. Probably women's greatest contribution to the world is found in the fact that they have inspired hundreds upon hundreds of men to climb from obscurity to prominent places in life. Possessed with a keen intuitive ability, women have recognized dormant powers in men and have aroused them to action. James Mackintosh, an English doctor, lawyer, philosopher and statesman, in a letter to a friend, beautifully described the character of his deceased wife. He wrote that she was "a woman who, by the tender management of my weakness, gradually corrected the most pernicious of them. She became prudent from affection; and though of the most generous nature, she was taught frugality and economy by her love for me. During the most critical period of my life she preserved order in my affairs, from the care of which she relieved me. She gently reclaimed me from dissipation, she propped my weak and irresolute nature and was perpetually at hand to admonish my heedlessness and improvidence. To her I owe whatever I am; to her whatever I will be."

This desire for significance differs from egocentricity in that it is directed in proper channels. It is constructive and is built upon sane hopes and possibilities. The woman does not merely flatter the man; she draws out his abilities and encourages him to direct them into specific accomplishments and achievements.

The quest for significance in marriage is largely determined by home environment and social standing in the community. If a woman marries a man of lower standing than herself and her circle of friends or acquaintances, she seeks in marriage to raise him to her standards. If this fails, she may desire to come down to his or avoid unhappiness by finding a substitute within the marriage, or even seek to have the union dissolved.

The desire for response and recognition in life is dynamic. It prompts mankind to seek an escape from moral failure and isolation. If this drive for significance is not realized, one is destined to lead a maladjusted life. Marriage is a natural and satisfactory outlet for the realization of these demands. It offers response to man's eagerness to make life meaningful. It protects him against insignificance and from a feeling of loneliness and insecurity in an indifferent world.

Any marriage which does not offer both partners an opportunity to find and develop significance through the union is destined to fail.

The third prominent urge in life is the need for love. This urge is so closely related to the urge for security and significance that it undergirds them. In the life of mankind, "love alone is primary."[1] Psychologists have discovered through analysis that "without love man's life is poverty-stricken, disordered and contrary to his own nature. Love is an indispensable necessity for the individual as for the communal life. . . There is a vital law of love to which the

1 Pfester, Oskar, The Psycho-Analytic Mind.

individual dare not refuse recognition either in the development of his own life or in the acquisition of the highest communal forms."[1]

Only the individual who has an organized love life can expect to have a well-ordered mind and controlled emotional stability. Love seeks outward expression, or better an attachment. It finds this expression in another person, who in reality becomes one with the lover so that "the twain become one flesh." No marriage can be successful that fails to satisfy this basic force. It demands sincerity, self-giving and response. Adler states that when considering love one must recognize primarily "that the interest of the whole, the interest of mankind, must always be involved. This interest is primary . . . The love problem is a task of two individuals . . . Each partner must be more interested in the other than himself. This is the only basis on which love and marriage can be successful."[2]

In this interest of one individual for the other there is not a domineering or superior attitude. Each makes the other feel that he is important and necessary to his very existence. When such an attitude is not evident there is no genuine love.

These three basic urges — the desire for security, significance and love — direct the individual toward matrimony. People marry because they want security. They must feel safe with and protected by the person they marry. Anything that will arouse suspicion or mistrust will undermine this goal. This is why fidelity and faithfulness are essential to a happy marriage. Marriage must add significance to life. There must be pride in the union. The individual should

[1] Pfester, Oskar, Some Applications of Psycho-analysis.
[2] Adler, Alfred, What Life Should Mean to You.

find in his marriage that which makes his life more important than it was when he was single. Fraud or deception will destroy this essential foundation for happiness. Love will find expression in affection and the sex life of the happy married couple. To guarantee this purpose in life one must be sure that he chooses the right life-partner.

THE CHOICE OF A LIFE-PARTNER

CHAPTER 2

The Choice of a Life-Partner

MARRIAGE is more than the choice of a mate. Animals seek mates, but man desires a partner. Animals are directed by instinct; man is guided by heart and mind. In marriage he seeks a partner, a companion who will remain with him throughout his life. If one enters into matrimony with the reservation "If I don't like it I'll get out of it," he is not seeking a partner but a temporary mate, and he makes the solemn vows of the marriage ceremony a mockery. Marriage vows are an oath taken by two people before God; the clergyman administering the oath on behalf of the Christian Church.

31

Since marriage means the choice of a companion and a home-partner for life, it is to be entered into with deliberation and forethought. The selection of a partner should be exercised with care. Marriages are not made in heaven, but on earth. The intelligent choice of a partner can make them heavenly. The contrary can produce hell on earth.

Matrimony offers unexplored territory for the discovery of love, but it also offers opportunity for the development of hatred.

Sherwood Eddy said that "probably the nearest most of us will ever come to heaven on this earth will be in the discovery of a life of deepening love in a happy home, and the nearest approximation to one's idea of hell will be found in being chained for life to the wrong person, where two lives irritate, thwart and defraud one another."[1] Possibly a couple such as that described in the closing words of this quotation would not stay "chained for life," but with the breaking of the chain often comes a broken heart.

Many make the wrong choice in marriage because they do not take time to deliberate. They marry in haste. Many hasty marriages are prompted by physical attraction. One makes a mistake if he ignores the importance of the physical aspect of marriage, but an equally grave error is to permit the physical to dominate completely.

There is a Bible story which tells that early in religious history physical attractiveness came to play a large part in marriage. Trouble followed. "It came to pass, when men began to multiply on the face of the earth, and daughters were born unto them, that the sons of God saw the daughters of men that they were fair; and they took them wives of all which they chose." The sons of God were spiritually-

[1] Eddy, Sherwood, **Sex and Youth.**

minded men, men of integrity and wisdom, but they married "the daughters of men," a worldly group whose members had one attribute: they were physically attractive. The men married without forethought or concern for posterity. The results of the unions were disastrous. The leaders proved themselves incompetent to make unbiased decisions, and God could not use them to lay the foundation for a strong and influential nation.

It is unwise to permit any one highly desirable trait to dominate one's selection of a partner. This one prize distinction may be the individual's only commendable trait and may not compensate for the qualities that are lacking. A pretty or handsome face soon loses its charm if it belongs to a disagreeable person. So it is with any one or two highly desirable traits that stand out against a barren background. The values of most people are composed of several small elements rather than one outstanding asset.

One needs to know something about the habits, the attitudes and purposes of an individual with whom he is planning to live in close confines and intimate relationships for life. A casual acquaintance is not a life-partner. You cannot tell anything about his interests or desires, his conception of a home, or how he responds to the demands and experiences of life. You may know a friend who married someone whom he scarcely knew, and they are a happy couple, but do not be governed by rare successes. Such a union has little likelihood of durability. If it does succeed, it is because the two people happen to possess the qualities which are necessary to make marriage a success. If they are to enjoy a happy marriage a couple should have common interests and tastes. To find a congenial life-partner will, therefore, demand time and patience, as there are many obstacles to overcome.

It is more difficult to find a life-partner in modern society than in simple rural life. Modern standards of marriage are not easily determined. The diversity of opinion is confusing and perplexing. Tradition is not an adequate standard. Young people no longer marry a person because "it is the natural thing to do." Fathers today cannot speak as formerly in advising their children regarding marriage partners.

The number of potential prospects is widened by an increased number of friends. The automobile has brought near-by towns together. A girl who contemplates marriage may be the only member of her family who knows her suitor. The couple court in an automobile instead of the family parlor.

Women are more independent than ever. A woman does not need to marry for a home. Sometimes, in fact, she provides a home for the man. She may be forced to give up a position, should she marry, which pays more than the potential husband could ever hope to earn. I recently asked a young lady if she planned to marry soon. Her reply was, "I am not yet making enough money to support a husband."

It is through a maze of problems, ultimate contradictions and unblazed trails that a young person must travel in his search for a permanent companion. What guidance may he hope to find to assist him in his quest?

It is impossible and unwise to enumerate all the qualities that one is to seek in his marital partner. Qualities are relative. They are determined by the various needs of the individuals. As there are different people, so there are different demands. These desired attributes or traits depend upon one's personality, individuality and training. **Regardless** of the person whom one marries, one will discover that someone he courted is, in some respects, superior to the person he married. The person not selected for a partner may, nevertheless, have more inferior traits and defects than the one chosen. If the person one intends to marry is eager to "make a go of marriage" he has the true psychological approach to matrimony. This attitude is fundamental.

The direction of their development is more important than what the two are at the time of marriage. Without evidence of this desire for perfection there is little hope for a happy union. The person you contemplate marrying may or may not have all the qualities you desire in a life-partner, but if he has the willingness to acquire them, he possesses the foundation of married partnership. The desire to co-operate will reveal itself in thoughtful acts and deeds which add to comfort and inspire confidence and companionship.

Among the reasons some men gave for being happily married was the fact that their wives were concerned about their physical comfort. "She washes my back," was a familiar statement. Some women attribute their happiness to the fact that "he gladly rubs my back."[1] Some people do not want their backs washed or rubbed, but they want their socks darned or their hair washed. These simple acts of consideration reveal a kindly attitude toward one's partner and a desire to add to his comfort and happiness. These demonstrations of kindness are evidences that two people are interested in each other's welfare.

"Important as sex life may be," says Hart, "in many cases the critical question is whether they [man and wife] are

[1] Burkhart, Roy, **From Friendship to Marriage.**

able to work as partners in creative harmony."[1] David Seabury writes, "What are the forces that make for unhappy marriages? Legion." He states, however, that "there is generally but one cause. Their natures are not basically harmonious."[2] There can be no harmony where there is lack of companionship, the clash of opposing interests, on conflicting purposes. The person you marry must be your bosom companion; he must share your interests and confidence and be able to encourage and inspire you. This relationship must give evidence that it will develop favorably with the passing of the years. Companionship, therefore, must be based on more than one trait. Interests need to be founded on something that will not grow monotonous in a few months. A person's attitude reflects his philosophy of life. It discloses itself in the way a wife and husband treat each other in private and in the presence of others. As you are shown consideration by an individual so are you considered by him.

A young girl may be determined to marry a man who appears undesirable to her friends and her parents. When asked if she thinks she is making a wise choice, she may answer, "I love him, and that is all that counts." The subject of love will be discussed later, but let it be said here that love demands facts not fancy, truth not error, reality not fiction. Love asks for a foundation on which to build. The girl needs to ask herself, "Why do I love him?" If his personality is offensive and his interests are contrary to hers, though she may think she loves him, he cannot be a companion to her. In marriage one seeks companionship.

Companionship, similar interests and an acceptable attitude are three qualities which are so closely related that the

1 Hart, Hornell, **Chart for Happiness.**
2 **Unmaking Our Mind.**

one cannot be complete without the other. Similar interests make companions and companions develop similar attitudes. One's attitude attracts companionship and interests color attitude. Where there are co-ordinating interests and similar attitudes the result is harmony. Where there is no harmony two cannot live happily together. Everyone, therefore, contemplating marriage should ask himself, "Can I live in harmony with this person? Do I enjoy his company? Have we similar interests? Do I appreciate his potentialities?" These builders of harmony are of such vital significance that they must be foundational in every contemplated marriage. Life seeks to find security, significance and love, and these fundamental attributes guarantee them. Examine them closely.

1. **Companionship.** Companionship between members of the opposite sex begins with a liking for the individual, then a feeling of security in his presence; a feeling which increases and adds significance to life. When the friendship fails to provide security, significance and love, it is broken. Between married people this satisfaction must reach a point where there is assurance of security, significance and love. When these are wanting, harmony ceases and strife arises. Such a marriage is destined for failure.

A man seeking a wife is consciously or unconsciously seeking a companion. Augustine wrote in his **City of God** that "If God had destined woman as man's master, He would have taken her from his head; if as his slave, He would have taken her from his feet; but as He designed her for his companion and equal He took her from his side." A man's wife is neither his master nor his slave; she is his companion. When she arises above or falls below him she has lost him as a husband. Victor Hugo was married fifty years to the same woman, but she was never his companion. It was Juliette Drouet that took the place of his wife in his heart. Juliette shared his interests and was his close companion throughout his life.

Marriages that have become renowned for their bliss were consummated by two close companions who lived together as married partners. Sir Samuel Romilly, according to record, found in his wife such true companionship that he "died of a broken heart" seven days after her death.

One of the happy literary men of history was Thomas Hood. He presented profound moral truths with a just balance of humor. His writings were "the delight of every boy and the instruction of every man who read them." He was a humorist and poet who lived and wrote on a sublime plane. "Though his wit was caustic, it was never coarse, and no single suggestion of impurity can be found in any of his writing."

Life was unkind to Hood, as it has been to many literary men. He associated himself with a business that failed. He refused to take advantage of bankruptcy but resolved to live a strict economic life so as to be able to pay his debts. Then followed a prolonged illness. He was finally granted a pension but lived only a year to enjoy it.

In the midst of adversity and hardship, Hood reflected a buoyant spirit. In marriage he had found a true companion. To his wife he attributed his happiness and success, and to her he wrote, "I never was anything, dearest, until I knew you; and I have been a better, happier and more prosperous man ever since." She was his counselor and companion. She read and copied his manuscripts and he corrected them at her suggestion. During his prolonged illness, Hood's faithful wife was at his bedside encouraging and assisting him in writing.

Regardless of the intellectual heights to which a man rises he still seeks companionship. Michael Faraday reached heights of scholarship as England's distinguished chemist and physicist. It was said of him that he was "one of the most brilliant experimentalists that science has ever known." But where did he find his happiness? After he was married twenty-eight years he wrote that his marriage was "an event which, more than any other, had contributed to his earthly happiness and healthy state of mind." His wife was the inspiring companion of his years.

In the choice of a partner look for a companion whose company you will enjoy increasingly as you learn to know him. If he is a true companion, you will be happy in his presence and lonesome in his absence. His disposition will be pleasing to you, and you will have a desire to be with him as long as you live. You will seek his opinion on various problems and be eager for his comments. What others say will have little effect upon you, for his words will be of major significance. Though you go places and do things together, the important consideration will not be the places or the event, but the fact that you are together. You will find yourselves growing together in thought and in fellowship. Each time you part or are separated you will look forward to the day when you have the opportunity to "talk things over again." You will have many subjects to discuss that were held in abeyance awaiting your friend's opinion.

The person who becomes your closest companion must be attractive to you; his disposition must be congenial and his personality pleasing. You will soon part if these qualities are not evident. Remember that a home is a home because it provides comradeship or companionship such as the world cannot offer. If the home fails to do this, a husband will go his way and a wife her way to find it. Wives eager for companionship become an easy prey to "smooth" men.

Companions maintain a kindly attitude toward each other. According to Shakespeare, kindness supersedes a woman's appearance. "Kindness in women, not their beauteous looks, shall win my love." Where there is kindness there is love. The kind are slow to take offense, willing to take advice, and have a desire to co-operate. When there is harmony there is love. Love is the union of those whose pattern of life is in harmony. Life seeks to find satisfaction and expression in love. This is basic to married life. Where there is true companionship there is harmony, and where there is harmony in marriage there is love. Be sure that the person you marry can be a companion to you and that you feel at home in his company. Edmund Burke could say, "Every care vanishes the moment I enter my own roof," because his wife was a true companion to him.

It is true that a married person will have other companions and friends, but there will be one of the opposite sex who will be superior to all others. That person will be your marital partner, if you have chosen wisely. You naturally desire to live with your best companion.

2. **Interests.** Those who have similar interests can live happily together. Individuals have peculiar interests of their own, and they need not forfeit them, but there must be predominant common interests between a man and his wife. One cannot detest the other's major interest but should appreciate, share and respect it. If a couple are to live happily as man and wife there must be complementary rather than clashing interests.

Sharing similar interests gives meaning and significance to life, and thus satisfies a basic urge. Interest in a person's objective is interpreted as interest in the individual. A wife who is a musician and married to a man who does not appreciate music will interpret his lack of interest in music as indifference to her. She may be heard to say, "He doesn't care what I do. He is not interested in my music."

It does not follow that only those who have the same interests should marry, but that one can and will appreciate the other's major interest and contribute to its enjoyment. If a woman marries an artist she need not be an artist, but she should have ability to appreciate art and her husband's work. Sharing of chief interests is essential to harmony.

William Blake was the son of a London hosier. At the age of twenty-three he became attracted to a girl sufficiently to ask for her undivided attention. She spurned his request. Heartbroken, Blake told his story to a simple market-gardener's daughter, Catherine Boucher. She showed him such understanding, interest and sympathy that he fell in love with her and married her. Only the wealthy women were educated, and poor Catherine could not even write her name. But the interest she manifested in Blake when he told her of his disappointment in love continued until his death. He taught her to read and write and to engrave. She became an apt student and acquired considerable skill in the art of engraving. She sat up nights working with her husband, and rambled with him into the countryside on walks covering thirty miles a day. To the poet, artist, engraver and painter, Catherine, whom Blake tenderly called "Kate", was "my shadow of delight." When he came to portray the face of Eve, an angel, a queen or the Madonna, it was only the face of "Kate" that he could see worthy of such honor. She was ever beside him as a counselor, associate and friend. Given to visions as he was, he shared every vision with her. The interest of Blake's wife in his work and in his aspirations was the one smooth path in his troubled life. Blake probably concluded, before he proposed to her, that a woman who would be interested in the heartache of a neglected lover would be interested in his lifework.

There is an element of truth in the statement by Oliver Wendell Holmes that "the brain-women never interest us like the heart-women." Men desire both assets in a wife, but if it is to be one without the other the heart-woman will win. The heart-woman, who makes an effort to understand and share her lover's interests, will not find it difficult to find a husband and remain married.

There should be sufficient mutual interest for a married couple to enjoy the same or similar amusements, so that if one wants to go camping he need not do so without the other.

A man's success depends to a remarkable degree upon the interest and encouragement of his wife. Keyserling[1] recommended that one should marry only that person who could assist him in accomplishing what he could not accomplish alone. No man or wife can build a happy home alone. United interests and co-operation are needed to beautify and make comfortable a newly-married couple's home.

If one considers the lives of those who became famous, he will find, in the vast majority of cases, that what brought fame to one was usually the work of two: the work of a man and his wife. John Stuart Mills said that his wife was in part the author of all that was best in his writings. It was with the eyes of his wife that the blind Geneva naturalist studied.

1 Keyserling, H., **The Book of Marriage.**

The French author, statesman and political philosopher De Tocqueville died at the age of fifty-four. When he was thirty he married an English woman, Mary Mottley. Though he and his wife were handicapped by their different nationalities as the Blakes were hampered by their difference in education, De Tocqueville could write, "Of the blessings which God has given to me, the greatest of all, in my eyes, is to have lighted on Marie." Nearing the end of life, he declared, "I could not go on with my task if it were not for the refreshing calm of Marie's companionship." His wife shared his interests and schooled herself to contribute to his success.

Potential home-partners must have common interests if for no other reason than to be saved from boredom. The woman who can talk only about herself or the neighbors will soon have no one to talk to but herself. The man who can relate nothing but what "happened at the office today" will discover an indifferent listener.

Interest must go beyond and be deeper than changing circumstances. A man may marry a girl who works with him in the same office. During the little time they have together they talk about the office. Then they marry, the girl ceases to work, and her husband takes a new position. Can they find common interests to discuss? One should be sure that his interests do not clash but are similar or supplementary to the interests of the person he desires to marry. Similar and shared interests make life significant and meaningful.

3. **Potentiality.** The term "potentiality" covers a wide area. It is used only for want of a better word to describe the basic desire for security. It does more than take cognizance of the present. It pries into the past and looks

toward the future. It takes inventory of one's capacities, ambitions and possibilities.

When one seeks a marital partner the desire for security will consciously or unconsciously demand a satisfactory answer. "Is this the right person for me to marry?" is an essential question prompted by the desire for security, which leads to an analysis and consideration of the facts. The thoughtful person wants a guarantee that the marriage will succeed. He weighs evidence for and against closing the contract. Those who marry hastily ignore this prerequisite, while others may sense its imperativeness and postpone marriage until it is too late to wed.

The desire for security causes a woman to ask, "Can he give me a home? Will I be happy? What of my future?" It prompts a man to ask such questions as: "Will she help me in my work? Will she be faithful to me? Will she be acceptable or agreeable to my parents and friends?"

To answer this urge for security in marriage, and satisfy it completely, one should compare his own background, his personality and philosophy of life with that of the prospective partner's.

1. **Background.** Physical and mental health will be considered under this heading. "Health," said Aristotle, "is more important than love." Whether it is more important or not, it is a positive factor in keeping love alive. One should know about the physical health of the parents of the espoused. If there have been deaths in the family caused by susceptibility to infectious diseases one should consult a competent physician before consenting to marriage. One should exercise caution in marrying children of parents suffering from mental diseases even though research in the

field of eugenics reveals that only a small proportion of the feeble-minded are children of feeble-minded parents.

When a young person selects a life-partner he is choosing a parent for his future children.

He should be convinced that no physical defect or mental incompetency is likely to be passed on to his children through the union. One should take into consideration the individual's race and religion, his relationship to his parents, his education and social standing, and the family's attitude toward each other and outsiders. The parents' attitude toward each other is often duplicated in the attitudes of their sons and daughters toward their life-partners. A son who cannot break away from his mother's "apron strings" and a daughter who has a father fixation and must always project "Daddy's" opinions and wishes into every conversation are likely to be unsuitable partners. In marriage a man shall "leave father and mother, and shall cleave to his wife: and they twain shall be one flesh. Wherefore they are no more twain, but one flesh." While respect for and congenial relationships with parents are necessary, there must be a loyalty to the marital partner which surpasses loyalty to the parents. It is necessary that a prospective bride know the attitude of her suitor's family toward her and her parent's attitude toward her fiancé and his family. More is involved in the relationship than appears on the surface. The congenial attitude of in-laws will do much to guarantee pleasant associations when members of both families are brought closely together. It is important that both families be consulted about matrimonial plans, and any objection raised by them should be given careful consideration. One has increased possibilities of enjoying a happy married life if the parents of both families consent to the union.

Common interests depend a great deal upon one's education and cultural background. Imagine the situation which exists when one who enjoys reading Shakespeare's works finds that the person he plans to marry is satisfied with nothing beyond the comic-book level. Elevating literature would be meaningless to the uneducated partner. Persons who are widely different in educational attainments must, inevitably, make more adjustments to achieve harmonious living than those who have the same educational background. Hart[1] discovered that "it is a poor risk for a college graduate to marry a person who failed to finish high school." Note that he said, " . . . who failed to finish high school." One may not be a high-school graduate because he was detained from school by powers beyond his control. The student who could not pass the examination or did not have the stamina to finish school is a poorer partner because he lacked the stability that the college graduate demonstrated. Questionnaires[2] have proved fairly conclusively that wives want their husbands to be older and to be superior in intelligence and education to themselves. Potential husbands, among college men, want their wives to have as much education as they, but not more. A woman wants a man with more intellectual strength than she possesses, whereas a man wants a woman with an extra share of beauty but not so much intellectual power as to make him appear ignorant. She can have beauty; he wants intelligence. The few studies made support the opinion that there are fewer failures among unions in which both man and wife are college graduates or have had college training than among marriages in which the partners never attended college. Education develops tolerance, imparts information, encour-

1 **Chart for Happiness.**
2 Rockwood, L. J., and Ford, M.E.N., **Youth, Marriage and Parenthood.**

ages culture and creates ability to "give and take." The ability to "give and take" or to be a "good sport" in the face of disappointed and thwarted plans is essential to a harmonious marriage.

One's social station is determined largely by his background. People usually marry within their own social group. Sadler is of this opinion: "One thing is sure: happy marriages are not going to result from unions of those who are too far separated in social standing, cultural attainment or natural endowment."[1] This point is well taken. Difference in social standing in itself creates a problem to be overcome. When the difference is marked it involves the choice of friends, acquaintances and interests. Women can marry beneath their social standing and lift their husbands to their level, but men find it difficult to enable wives below their social standing to be accepted by their group. Society is more reluctant to accept women than men into exclusive fellowship.

Couples who do not marry too far above or too much below their social position have increased opportunities for happiness. One's conception of a home, his attitude toward financial problems, and his choice of amusements and intimate friends are determined largely by his accustomed social standard. When one marries too far up or down the scale he must make numerous adjustments, and the most serious involves finances, the demon that causes countless quarrels in otherwise happy homes. Only one who marries a wealthy person will be guaranteed financial security, but there must be more than money in this union to satisfy the basic desire for security. The wealthy person must consider the suitor's purpose. "Does he want me or my money?" will be the

1 Sadler, Wm., and Lena, **The Sex Life.**

expressed or unexpressed fear. When motives are questioned there can be no satisfying sense of security.

The next important factor in choosing the proper marital partner is to evaluate his philosophy of life. What is his attitude toward sex, marriage, religion and people in general? What does he expect from life, and what does he resolve to contribute to it? His philosophy of life is determined largely by his personality traits. Is he an introvert or an extrovert? An introvert lives within himself. He is attracted to ideas, discoveries and people who share this interest. He is interested in people because of the ideas they possess, and not because they are people. The extrovert is the opposite. He likes people because they are people, and he is not happy apart from them. He is not interested in "why's and wherefore's". As long as people are happy he is not concerned about the mechanics of happiness. He does not ask, "What makes people happy?" but says, "Let's make everyone enjoy himself." It is natural that the attitudes of the extrovert and the introvert toward home life would conflict. But the redeeming feature is that few of us are extreme introverts or extroverts. These two types overlap. The important fact for a suitor to remember is that the interests of a decided introvert are foreign to those of an extrovert. There would be little intimate companionship, few interests and a scarcity of corresponding purposes between the two. The two live in different worlds. One inhabits a world of self; the other moves in a world of people.

Schopenhauer[1] contended that opposites are attracted to one another more than people with similar personalities. In this he has been proved to be incorrect as he was in his contention that "blondes prefer dark persons, or brunettes,

1 The Philosophy of Schopenhauer.

but the latter seldom prefer the former" or that he "who marries from love must live in sorrow. . . Happy marriages are well known to be rare." Statistics show that the majority of people marry those who follow their own interests and that a person likes to be with one who is of his own status and kind. We feel at home with those who share our common ideals and standards.

All attempts to unite people of conflicting types in intimate companionship fail; the materialist and the idealist, the cynic and the conservative, the skeptical and the appreciative, the demanding and the sympathetic, the rigid and the liberal, the sexually active and the passive, the unscrupulous and the puritanical have almost unsurmountable obstacles to overcome if they are to achieve unity, and only by constant compromise can they live harmoniously. There can be no satisfying comradeship, sharing of interests and feeling of security in the presence of a person decidedly contrary in temperament and philosophy of life, or one who holds convictions and standards opposed to those of the other. One of the fields in which this will cause much dissension is the realm of moral principles. "The most indispensable qualification in a husband or a wife, and one which is most frequently made of little importance, is a good moral and religious character. Without it the most splendid natural and acquired gifts will fail."

One needs to weigh the evidence for and against an individual before rushing into marriage with him. One must demand more than physical and intellectual satisfaction in marriage. The spiritual and moral aspects must also be satisfied. Where there is love only the spiritual can purify and sustain it, for "love is of God."

Florence Nightingale's evaluation of her moral nature

persuaded her to remain single. "I have an intellectual nature which requires satisfaction, and that would find it in him. I have a passional nature which requires satisfaction, and that would find it in him. I have a moral, an active, nature that requires satisfaction, and would not find satisfaction in him." In similar words Dr. Groves advises, "Although there are many virtues that one would like to find in any candidate for matrimony, there is one that we must look for sincerely; if it is absent, turn away from an alliance that is almost sure to fail." That one virtue is, according to Dr. Groves, moral qualities.[1]

Concerning every definite difference in thinking and custom found in a possible mate the suitor should ask himself, "What does this mean to me and my future happiness?" Possibly what he feels he can ignore or abandon easily he discovers too late has become a vital part of his life. One must consider the matter carefully before he agrees to adopt a contradictory attitude toward certain accustomed practices or before he dismisses them as meaningless. The purpose of courtship is to discover a partner who "wears well" in all kinds of weather, who brings out your best when you are at your worst, and whose similar interests tend to increase companionship and the sharing and strengthening of a common philosophy of life. Such a person is your life-partner. He fulfills your basic desire for significance, security and love. Marry him.

[1] Groves, E. R., "When He Comes A-Courting," **Good Housekeeping, Sept., 1938.**

HOW TO WIN THE ONE YOU'D WED

CHAPTER 3

How to Win the One You'd Wed

The one you would like to marry may or may not be known to you. You may have a mental conception of the one to whom you would give your heart but you have not met him, or you may know the person but be unable to determine his attitude toward marriage. Both of these situations will be discussed in this chapter.

You may meet the person of whom you have a mental image by putting yourself "in circulation" and affording yourself an opportunity to meet members of the opposite sex. If you are looking for a sport, frequent beaches, golf courses, clubs and other places where sports of both sex circulate freely. If you desire a Christian companion, attend religious youth camps, conventions and Christian activities. You can meet the person whose friendship you desire by going where he dwells, and to do so is not impudence but common sense.

I recall a girl whose ambition was to marry a minister. She enrolled in a theological school before she found the mate she desired. In her senior year she realized her purpose by marrying one of the students of the first-year class.

After you participate in the activities that appeal to the type of person you want to marry, you will fail to reach your goal if you make your purpose too obvious. Do not confide even in a close friend. Show first an interest in the activities, not the actors, but don't neglect either. Your purpose is noble. It is two-fold. You want a happy home and a married life that will bring joy to you and your partner, and you are interested in the activities with which you have associated yourself. If it becomes obvious that you are man-or woman-hunting, you may offend the members of your own sex and become unpopular with them. A girl who is unpopular with girls will be unpopular with men. Women want to know the man who is liked by other men. They will ask their acquaintances, who know him, for an introduction. The more popular a person is the more opportunity he will have to meet the right person.

There are a number of elements in popularity. Troxel[1] lists four. They are pertinent to this discussion. He says that these four attributes make a girl popular: (1) talent; (2) rare beauty; (3) pleasing personality; (4) possession of wealth.

He places talent first and wealth last. Two of these demands we can control and the others we may inherit.

1 Troxel, Thomas, **Ways to Successful Matrimony for Women.**

Man's conception of beauty varies so widely that "rare beauties" are few. No sensible girl wants a man to marry her for beauty or riches alone. The same is true of a handsome man. He wants more than a woman who is interested in his appearance and possessions. The two requirements that remain are within the grasp of all. By talent Troxel means a special ability in a particular field. One seeking a home-partner should, therefore, increase his social skills and accomplishments. The individual with no special interest will find it difficult to interest the right person.

History shows us that the women of "rare beauty" and the handsome men had more than mere external beauty to offer their suitors. "Being popular," Jonathan[1] tells men, "means liking people and showing them that you do. It means knowing what to do and how to do it in the clever, smooth way. Also, it means standing on your own feet, making your own decisions, solving problems as they come — in stride. And being popular means being a gentlemen." This requirement demands talent and personality. This quality some might call "It." Cleopatra, the greatest woman love-maker of history, knew how to inspire men. She praised them for their achievements. When she was only seventeen she pierced Caesar's heart. She caused Mark Anthony to divorce Octavia who was a "rare beauty" to marry her. The tactics of Cleopatra are not to be commended or duplicated but she proves that the girl who has neither rare beauty nor wealth nevertheless has a strong weapon to slay the hearts of men. Sir Walter Raleigh had more than a handsome appearance to win the favor of England's stern

[1] Jonathan, Norton, **Gentlemen Aren't Sissies.**

queen. He had good manners and a winsome personality. Good manners usually accompany a pleasing personality.

Acquire and develop an interest in the activities that appeal to the person whom you wish to marry. This is the first requirement. After you have done this, attract the individual to you. Absorb yourself in the interests of the one you admire and express your admiration for his proficiency in this sport or activity. Recognize the quality in the individual you admire and let him know that you do. This practice is feasible for men and women alike.

Strive to develop a pleasing personality, since personality attracts. What is personality? It is difficult to define, but you know when a person does or does not possess it. According to Dr. May,[1] "Personality might be characterized as that total organization of reaction tendencies, habit patterns and physical qualities which determine the individual's social effectiveness." It is the "external manifestations and internal feeling of the individual." People see us, respond to our physical appearances, our behavior, our attitude and our visible expressions; we respond to them. Our attitude toward them, toward life and toward ourselves forms the basis of their conception of our personalities.

Can you feel at ease in the presence of others? If not, why? Find the difficulty and correct it. By doing this you develop your personality. Do you offend people easily? Seek the reason and instead of brooding over it, attempt to remedy it, and by this process you build your personality.

Possibly one of the clearest ways to define personality is to look at the traits possessed by those who have pleasing personalities. "The personality," says Dr. McCarthy,[2] con-

1 May, M. A., **The Foundation of Personality.**
2 McCarthy, Ralph, **Safeguarding Mental Health.**

sists of the sum total of all the natural and acquired traits that the individual possesses. It includes the body with its charm or lack of it, the mental powers of intelligence, imagination and will, the emotional make-up, the impulses, tendencies, aspirations, habits and attitudes which an individual has either inherited or formed through experience."

When all these traits working harmoniously supplement each other, the individual has an integrated personality. Therefore it is not only necessary that an individual possess certain traits but that they work together harmoniously. Their integration governs the greatness of that personality. When these are neglected we say that a man has possibilities but a negative personality. Personalities are built.

Dr. W. F. Thomas found that the characteristics which men like in women, and listed in the order of importance as given by seven hundred college students, are: beauty, intelligence, cheerfulness, congeniality of interests and sex attraction. Women prefer men who have intelligence, consideration, kindliness, cheerfulness and mannerliness. All those traits except beauty are possible to develop and are personality assets. Beauty can also be acquired to some degree by the possession of the other attributes. People dislike those who possess the opposite of these traits: selfishness, pessimism, deceptiveness and affectedness. Cason[1] found that the source of annoyance to others is primarily lack of manners, i. e., "belching, bragging, cheating, continually criticizing, failing to listen, etc." The popular person makes other people feel important, avoids causes of offense and shows consideration.

A person must first attract the attention of the one he

[1] Cason, H., **Common Annoyances.**

would win. A cheap or bold manner will, however, offend the normal person or misrepresent your purpose. There is nothing that will attract attention to you more than a pleasing personality, which is nothing more than attractive conduct. Emerson wisely stated that "a beautiful behavior is better than a beautiful form." Anyone can cultivate good behavior, and to do so is to enhance one's personality.

The second group who would win a home partner, already knows the individual he wants to marry, but he is not in a receptive mood. The situation is more complicated for a girl than a man. She has to wait for the proposal of the young man, but she can lead up to it. Swedenborg maintained that the woman was the aggressor in love. Nevertheless, it is not advisable for her to offer a formal proposal of marriage. What is to be a girl's technique in winning the husband of her choice?

1. **She should let it be known that she is willing and ready to marry before she discourages her prospective suitor.** A girl who talks about a career or working for her Ph. D. degree is saying to a young man that she is "out of circulation" until she has attained her goal. A girl may state her ambition but she can add, "My plans are subject to change." The gentle hint will suffice to let him know that something may be more important to her than her career or attainments.

2. **She should study men and their interests — not one man's interests but the ambitions of men.** Ruskin said that "a girl worth anything ought to have always half a dozen or so of suitors under vow to her." He meant that a girl should not know a man but a number of men who thought highly of her. Men are interested in a girl who is interested in them and yet doesn't "chase" them.

She should discover what a man likes to talk about. He wants to talk about himself. To encourage his doing so, she should discover what interests him. His interests are a part of him, and as he discusses them he tells about himself.

An alert girl was talking to a young man who had a companion whom she liked. She asked "Where is your pal, Jack?" "He is at the opera," was the reply. Then he explained how "crazy" Jack was about the opera. The young lady started to attend the performances alone. Jack discovered her presence and invited her to be his guest. She asked him to explain the opera story to her. This association led to dates, until she discovered that he was not the man she wanted. But she became interested in the opera, and eventually, through Jack, met another opera fan, whom she married.

3. **She should be genuine.** You may hear men say of a girl, "I like her because she is real." Don't try to hide your emotions or be ashamed of them, but let it be known that you can control them. It is not natural for a girl to be mannish, so act and dress in a feminine manner. Most men want a woman to be a lady. They want to be sure that the girl they marry lets them "wear the trousers." They like to "dress" their wives in beautiful clothes. The average man will wear an old suit to buy a "pretty" dress for the woman he loves. He derives more satisfaction from seeing his wife attractively attired than from being well dressed himself.

4. **She should act kindly at all times.** No man wants a grouchy or moody wife. He knows that such a woman will nag. Though he changes himself, he wants her to be as steadfast as the Rock of Gibraltar.

A girl who cultivates a kindly attitude attracts men. In

the time of sorrow or disappointment they will seek her and propose to her. She will become their confidante in time of trouble.

There is nothing that pays larger dividends in potential husbands than kindness. This is why a man's mind turns back to his mother or grandmother in time of adversity; they were kind in days of trouble.

Identify yourself with a man's happiness, success and enjoyment, and you will be the first person he will want to tell about his successes or his failures.

5. **She should observe a high moral standard.** Regardless of anything you may be told about the acceptability of a double standard, question it carefully. Men still prefer the girl who is pure but not prudish. Troxel states that "every type of man admires a virtuous girl. A girl can be a good sport and at the same time maintain a certain dignity and decency that will lead men on to a point of her own choosing." Keep your standards high and even those who have low standards will come to you. A man likes to be able to say of the girl he marries what Edmund Burke wrote concerning his wife: "No person of so few years can know the world better; no person was ever less corrupted by the knowledge of it." Studies still reveal that the girl of character is still high on the scale of happy marriage. A man wants to marry a girl who will build up his self-respect. Consciously and unconsciously he will seek the intimate companionship of, and marry, such a girl. Remember—no girl can heighten a man's self-respect if she does not have it herself. Goodness in women has a profound appeal to men.

Let a man know that you feel the call of worldly interest as much as he does, but that you have established boundary lines over which you will not pass. This tells him that you have passion and human interests but more: self-control and character. This will give you an opportunity to declare clearer than you can say that only the man who marries you will receive your full affection. Remind the man that he will marry some day and speak of the type of husband he will want to be. Continue to remind him, when suitable occasions arise, that he will marry. Drop the thought of marriage into his mind and let him know that you want him happily married. A high moral standard offers an excellent opportunity to present to a man an appeal for a happy married life.

If a girl states her attitude clearly without condemning anyone, especially the man or other girls, she will be amazed by the changed attitude of a man who makes unreasonable advances toward her. It is the "holier than thou" attitude, which in itself is a vice, that makes the pure girl prudish. Let the young man whom you would like to marry know that your affection and love are reserved until marriage, and that in the interest of your happiness and his you have taken a stand that is not going to be changed though it may demand self-restraint and self-control. A man will admire your frankness, your genuineness and your determination. These qualities will make it easy for him to ask who that man might be. You can easily tell him that you like him a great deal. Shakespeare says of a woman that "there is a language in her eye, her cheek, her lips." Let that language speak.

When in the Navy I heard hundreds upon hundreds of men talk about their girl friends. When I asked, "When are you going to marry?" they answered, "Not now." Further questioning often revealed that though they liked to go out with "anybody" they would not marry "just any girl." Men were willing to overlook many faults in a girl but they were suspicious of the girl who was "easy to make."

6. **She should prepare for marriage.** Let it be known that you think of marriage. A high moral standard will introduce the subject. Other relative themes will present themselves. Seize them. If you are a student, take a course that will prepare you for home-making and, incidentally, let your interest be known. Young women have been warned not to be too aggressive, and that admonition is wise, but don't be afraid to let it be known that you are preparing yourself for marriage, that you consider marriage a life-job and that you are training and preparing yourself to enter it.

7. **She should not be a "clinging vine."** Let a fellow know that you like him above others, that you enjoy every minute of his company, but that he does not have a monopoly on your time until he has proposed. Do not always be ready to go out whenever he calls. Occasionally tell him that you are sorry but that you have other plans. Make him happy in your company and let him know that you enjoy his company but that he can never be sure of your "doing nothing" until he comes. Do not tell where you are going or with whom, but merely state that, although you are sorry, you can't go out with him on a moment's notice. This action will produce one of two results: it will give him an opportunity to give you up gracefully if that is his wish or it will make him eager to secure a monopoly on your dates if he loves you. He will be obliged to decide; if he has a delightful time with you, he had better "talk business." You can let him know that you enjoy his company

above all others but that you will not pine or fret if he chooses to neglect you. A man wants to think he has captured you and not that he has to marry you because you think he should.

Here are suggestions which you will apply if you desire to win a certain young lady for your wife.

1. **Declare your intentions.** It is easier for a man to win the girl he wants to marry, as he can make overtures that a girl can't. He can ask a girl to spend an evening with him whereas a girl cannot always extend such an invitation gracefully.

A man still offers the proposal to marry, and not the girl. How should he express the desire? According to John Ruskin he should do this when he meets the girl he wants to marry: "When a youth is fully in love with a girl, and feels that he is wise in loving her, he should at once tell her so plainly, and take his chances bravely, with other suitors. No lover should have the insolence to think of being accepted at once, nor should any girl have the cruelty to refuse at once, without severe reason."

A man should not hesitate to let a girl know how he feels toward her. It is never wise to assume that the girl knows. Caution should be exercised in making statements and promises that one is not prepared to substantiate, but the man who sees in a woman his potential wife and is eager to know her better before making a proposal should make known his interests. In many instances the girl grows cold toward a suitor because she did not know his intentions, no man should assume that she knew he would marry her some day. She had no indication that the man even contemplated marriage, and "it is as easy to count atomies as to resolve the propositions of a lover." If you would win the girl you want, tell her your interests early and wait patiently for her to make up her mind.

2. **Don't forget romance.** Women talk and live romance. They admire the romantic manner and do not like to feel that they are selected to be wives as commodities are inspected and chosen. Make the proposal unusual, and offer it under favorable conditions, in an environment that encourages romance. Mrs. Browning gives this advice to young men who plan to propose: "Lead her from the festive boards, point her to the starry skies."

An intelligent approach to marriage does not demand that it be lifted out of the realm of romance. The emotional aspect cannot and need not be ignored by one who strives to maintain an intelligent approach to marriage. Instead of detracting from romance, it adds to it. Groves[1] states, "The situation of the student who attempts to anticipate in an intelligent way the marriage relationship is like that of the traveler who before entering a foreign land for the first time tries to get all the information he can that will make his journey comfortable, his route well chosen and his contact with the people fruitful. As a result of his preparation he multiplies the enjoyment and the profit of his visit."

A girl will not appreciate a proposal that has only scientific appraisal. She will ask, "Why do you want to marry me?" She will not be highly elated by an answer that is purely rational and void of emotion. The man who states that he cannot live without such an adorable creature will win. When Moses Mendelssohn, a hunchback, fell in love with beautiful Frunitze Guggenheim, he realized that his physical condition was offensive to the young girl, so he awaited the opportune moment to propose. Without arguing

1 Groves, Ernest R., **Marriage.**

the reason why she should marry him he waited until one day she asked him, "Do you believe marriages are made in heaven?" "Yes," was his answer. Then he said, "At birth an angel calls out the name of your partner. Mine was a hunchback, but I cried, 'O Lord, a girl hunchback may become bitter. Give the hunchback to me and let her be handsome and well formed.'" Frunitze smiled, gave him her hand and said, "Yes."

You may hear this question asked concerning a girl: "Why did she refuse that intelligent man and marry that individual?" The answer may be that the intelligent man tried to make his proposal too intellectual. A proposal must direct its appeal to the heart.

Tell her in beautiful words what she means to you. "That man that hath a tongue, I say, is no man if with his tongue he cannot win a woman."

A man will receive his reward who does not delay in letting a girl know his favorable attitude toward her, but he should not be too aggressive in his wooing. He should wait to propose when the setting is convenient for a favorable response.

3. **Be mannerly.** Through a little effort anyone can acquire good manners. Good manners are indispensable if others are to feel at ease in your presence. Fear of what you might do or say is removed, and this situation encourages relaxation and comfort. The mannerly person does not talk about himself unduly but encourages others to talk. He protects a woman from embarrassing moments and situations. He is specific about dates and arrives punctually. He is well groomed and pays attention to "little things" that add to his personal appearance. He does not take his girl "for granted." He demonstrates thoughtfulness in

bestowing little courtesies and considerations on her. There
are three excellent books on this subject in addition to that
by Emily Post. These contain invaluable suggestions and
and are listed in the bibliography.

4. **Be pleasant.** A girl will marry a man who is pleasant
much sooner than she will a man who has some other virtue,
important though it be. A pleasant disposition tells a girl
much that she wants to know about the man she contemplates marrying. It shows that he has matured, that he is
not always thinking about himself but has interests in
others, and that he is easy to live with. The pleasant person
makes life happy for another. He wears well. If his
pleasantness is genuine he can take disappointment and
rebuff. He has learned to see beyond little and trivial events
to the great values that abide.

A girl will say of a pleasant person, "He's lots of fun."
She will enjoy his company so much that she will think
seriously before she says "No" to a proposal that might
remove him from her friendship.

People like to meet a pleasant person, and so a girl takes
pride in introducing a congenial man to others. He will add
charm to any occasion, create pleasant situations where
dullness may arise, and bring assurance where fear may
prevail.

A man is pleasant who is optimistic, agreeable and con-
siderate. Usually he enjoys excellent health, which is an
important asset in a marriage partner.

The pleasant person may have as many unpleasant
situations to meet as the grouch, but the former has trained
himself to look for the best in people and in situations. He
has acquired this virtue through practice, self-control and
discipline. "Few are qualified to shine in company, but it

is in most men's power to be agreeable," said Dean Swift. A girl feels reasonably sure that she can be happy with an agreeable man, and she wants to avoid quarreling.

Men and women contemplating marriage should pay attention to the following qualifications.

1. Make yourself attractive to your prospective suitor. Take an inventory of your habits, manners and personal characteristics.

Find that which offends, irritates or causes lack of interest and correct it immediately. Mention to the individual you love the traits which you have discovered. Do not let it be known, however, that you anticipate his reaction, but state the fault you have discovered in yourself and declare that you want assistance in correcting it. Be open to further suggestions from your lover. It is better for you to discover your defects than to have your prospective mate enumerate them for you. You will be loved for your initiative, candor and determination to make progress. Unconsciously you will tell your espoused that he or she brings out your best. It is a cherished honor to bring out the best in another person.

2. Do not patronize. No one wants to be patronized or to have the one he loves maintain a condescending attitude. No man or woman wants another person to "look down" on him. Usually, when one is better educated or in possession of more wealth than another, there is a supersensitiveness to a condescending air. Lord Chesterfield advised, "Abhor a knave and pity a fool in your heart, but let neither of them unreasonably see that you do." Any person seeking to win a marriageable partner should exercise care that there is no evidence of a condescending attitude toward anyone.

3. Be extravagant with genuine praise. Look for ad-

mirable traits which you can truly commend and express
your admiration for them. Refer to them frequently. The
virtuous and industrious wife of which Solomon wrote had
a motive for her diligence: "Her children arise up, and call
her blessed; her husband also, and he praiseth her." Praise
is not only sweet music to the ears of a woman but to a
man as well. Strong cords indeed are required to keep him
from the woman who delights him with the enticing music
of praise.

Praise is a powerful instrument. It is not to be used to
deceive, but to encourage. It will give fertility to a seed of
possibility that is almost dormant and cause it to grow
strong and powerful. It will cause men and women to do
strange and wondrous things. When a lover whispers or
proclaims words of praise about and in the presence of one
held dear, mankind cries, "One good deed, dying tongueless,
slaughters a thousand, waiting upon that: our praises are
our wages."

The one who will marry the person of his choice must
learn to discover his qualities, his potentialities and
strengthen them with encouragement, counsel and praise.

THE AGE AT WHICH TO MARRY

CHAPTER 4

The Age at Which to Marry

The problem "At what age should one marry?" is as old as reason. The early Hebrews answered the question for their children and selected mates for their sons whether they were mere children or middle-aged adults. The ancient Gauls thought it a disgrace to marry early, whereas the Chinese considered it a dishonor for a girl of twelve not to be married and they were embarrassed if a son of sixteen had no wife. The Greek scholar Plato contended that thirty was the ideal age at which a man should marry and that his wife should be ten years his junior. Aristotle reasoned that a man of thirty was too young to wed and that he should be thirty-seven. He believed also that his bride should be

eighteen. Aristotle did not follow his own advice. He
married at the age of thirty-six and his bride was not
eighteen. Both Plato and Aristotle were more concerned
about the welfare of the State than individual happiness in
marriage.

Love does not always consider one's age an important
factor in matrimony. This is evident when one observes the
age at which famous men married. Shakespeare became a
groom at the age of eighteen, Ben Johnson at twenty-one,
Benjamin Franklin and Wolfgang Mozart at twenty-four
and Sir Walter Scott at the age of twenty-six. George
Washington and Lord Byron chose brides when they were
twenty-seven. William Penn was single until he was twenty-eight; Robert Burns married at thirty. Geoffrey Chaucer
chose a wife when he was thirty-two; William Wordsworth,
at thirty-three. Martin Luther did not marry until he
was forty-two, and John Wesley waited until he was forty-
seven.

No one is wise in assuming that because some famous
person or acquaintance married early or late in life and is
happy that others following his example may anticipate the
same results. T. R. Malthus advised late marriages so as to
limit the number of births, and Hitler recommended early
marriages to insure the number of children that German
women could bear.

A harmonious marital relationship demands that the
partners consider the problem of children, but this
important issue must be a determining factor in deciding
the age at which one should marry only as it relates itself
to the mother's health and that of the child. The biological
side of marriage is only one of the many important aspects.
The physical, social, emotional, economical, mental and

spiritual demands must also be considered if a happy marriage is to be achieved.

Some of the arguments advanced in favor of marrying young are these:

1. **An early marriage forestalls promiscuousness.** It can be argued that if a couple meet while they are in their middle teens and marry in their late teens, they are man and wife before they feel the impact of the sex urge. After marriage they have little desire to be promiscuous as they were never tempted to practice illicit sex relationships.

2. **It is easy for young people to make adjustments.** This argument maintains that an early marriage enables a young couple to form a pattern of life before they have matured. This means that there are fewer habits to break and personal ambitions to conquer. The family is the predominant unifying factor in their lives.

3. **Early marriage reduces the hazards of childbirth since a young person recovers more quickly from illness.** There is less danger that the mother will lose her life at the birth of her child. Some scholars[1] contend that the children of comparatively young mothers have an advantage in longevity and eminence over those born of older parents. The most favorable age is that at which most American children are born, that is, when the mother is not under twenty and not more than twenty-nine.

4. **Children born to young mothers and fathers have the advantage of understanding parents.** Such mothers and daughters share numerous interests, and the fathers and sons have much in common.

1 Huntington, Ellsworth, **Seasons of Birth.**
1 Lorimer, Frank, and Osborn, Frederick, **Dynamics of Population.**

There are serious objections to these four arguments, especially those in support of teen-aged marriages:

1.   **The person whose morals are dependent upon sexual exhaustion is likely to be a problem.** There may be long months of illness or absence on the part of one's mate. What would keep the one who has wandering tendencies from being promiscuous at such a time? Love and devotion are more important in marriage than the desire to satisfy a biological urge.

2.   **Young people can make adjustments more readily than older people, but they have more demands made upon them which require attention.** A teen-aged marriage may be a union in which one or the other is immature and does not know what he or she wants. An early marriage increases the number of adjustments to be made, so that one becomes bewildered and confused by the multiplicity of problems. Youth's tastes change with age, and these changing interests and aims add to the problems of adjustments. One may reason, **I never knew what it was to be free,** and decide to exercise his freedom. I know of such a case. After twelve years of marriage, a young man with no grievance against his wife decided to divorce her. His reason was: "I want to enjoy my freedom. I married when I was too young."

3.   **The argument that the marriage of young people is a guarantee of the mother's welfare in childbirth and of the health of the child is worthy of consideration.** If the prospective mother has not reached physical maturity or if she is delicate, child-bearing can be serious. However, unless the couple's parents can help them financially it would be difficult for teen-aged parents to finance the proper care that mother and child should receive.

4.   **It is true that young parents can "grow up" with

their children, but if the father is young he may be so concerned with obtaining an education or earning a living that he will have little time to spend with his children. It is possible that grandparents enjoy their grandchildren because they did not have time to play and frolic with their own little sons and daughters.

Opinions offered against early marriage should be considered carefully. Some dangers are these:

1. **Early marriage tends to be influenced by the physical.** This is a serious danger and should be avoided. A young girl in her teens is perhaps more attractive than she will ever be. She is full of life, carefree and happy. To young men and old alike she is irresistible. Youth needs to ask the question, "Why do I want to marry now? Because of physical attraction? Because of the sex urge?" A young man or young woman who permits the physical to predominate in governing an early marriage is inviting trouble. It is wise to teach one's self a lesson in self-control and restraint. Let the mind supplement the emotions. Be certain of your motives by careful deliberation.

A marriage based on strong physical attraction and urges has many obstacles to its success. In the first place, such a marriage is founded on a changing ego rather than on lasting value. Disappointment, fault-finding and discord will inevitably arise. There must be an affinity of spirit—not merely a pretty or handsome face—to hold a marriage together. That which makes marriage beautiful is unseen. It is something within the individual, a strange charm, which unites two happy hearts.

Older men are not free from the danger of being influenced by the charm of the physical. Statistics show that the older a man becomes the younger the bride he selects. But that is another problem which will be considered later.

2. **Young people are inexperienced.** They tend, as a whole, to be guided by impulses rather than reason. The mature deliberate, whereas youth acts. Inexperience may lead a youth into serious difficulties in establishing and maintaining a proper and wholesome relationship with in-laws and parents. The sense of obligation and responsibility involved in marriage may not be appreciated fully by one who is very young.

There is also the question of limited experiences, which make it difficult to choose a partner wisely. How can a young person, who has most of his decisions made for him, whose problems are often anticipated and solved by his parents, make the most important choice of his life wisely? If he could not choose what was best for him as a son, how can he demonstrate sudden wisdom in one of the most serious and sacred decisions of his life?

3. **Early marriage frequently results in lack of opportunity for social development.** Modern research has proved that men and women who have had the opportunity of knowing a wide variety of friends tend to choose better partners and enjoy more marital happiness than those who have been denied the privilege of wide experiences. The former find it easier to meet and adapt themselves to another's way of life than the latter. A too early marriage does not afford opportunity to know and appreciate various types of personalities.

4. **Early marriage may interfere seriously with a man's financial and educational plans or life work.** There is, however, more than one element to consider in this assertion. Married students often achieve the best grades in school,

and young husbands are more efficient than older men in industry and business. Statistics show that income has little to do with marital happiness. Terman[1] found no correlation between family income and the marital happiness score. What he did discover was that financial limitations detracted from one's joy of living, which differs from marital happiness. Charles G. Woodhouse's[2] study supported Terman's. He found that the problem of income and its administration was not a decisive factor in happy or unhappy marital relationships. The Burgess-Cottrell[3] study shows little or no relationship between the income of a couple and their marital happiness. Dr. Robert C. Angell made a study of the effect of financial depression on family solidarity. There is nothing in his findings to show that reduced incomes produce marital unhappiness. The effects of finances on happiness depend upon the character of the individual concerned. These studies lead to the conclusion that there are happy and unhappy people in both the low and high income brackets. The possession of material things does not cause marital happiness nor does the lack of them cause unhappiness. The state of mind, the emotional maturity and the moral fortitude of those concerned — these are the decisive factors in a happy marriage.

It is easily proved that early marriage does not prevent mental development and growth or cause one to settle down in a monotonous routine of life, but the early appearance of children restricts the freedom of the parents, especially if insufficient funds make it impossible to employ a maid. A number of children born in close succession will make the married life of any couple restricted and arduous. Fre-

1 Terman. Lewis M., **Psychological Factors in Marital Happiness.**
2 Social Forces, VIII, 1930.
3 Burgess, E. W., and Cottrell, Leonard S., **Predicting Success or Failure in Marriage.**

quently one sees a young woman of twenty with two or three children who tries to be a wife, a nurse, a maid and a mother. This is difficult even for a mature woman, and has a tendency to make a young person appear older. The responsibility may, and often does, create disharmony and restlessness.

To anticipate and prepare for such a reaction is an excellent way to guard against these undesirable results.

People who marry late in life find it difficult to make satisfactory adjustments. They find it difficult to exercise tolerance as judgments and standards are already fairly established. Those who are older than thirty-eight find it hard to reconcile themselves to the demands of marriage, but have less difficulty than those who are exceedingly young. It is wiser to wait than to rush into marriage if one desires happiness.

Divorce is more frequent among the couples who marry below the age of nineteen than among those who are married in their late thirties. Marriages involving the very young are extremely unstable and result in separation, desertion, promiscuity, annulment and divorce.

Scientific investigation shows that when marriages are contracted when either partner is under twenty there is difficulty in finding marital happiness. A similar situation prevails when a husband is older than forty and a wife is more than thirty-five. Anyone who wishes to consult other authorities in this field should familiarize himself with the scientific studies suggested below.[1]

David Seabury quotes a prominent judge in New York Family Court as saying that "one of the major causes of

1 Burgess, E. W., and Cottrell, L. S., Predicting Success or Failure in Marriage.
1 Davis, K. D., Factors in the Sex Life of Twenty-two Hundred Women.
1 Hamilton, G. V., and Macgowan, Kenneth, What Is Wrong with Marriage?
1 Terman, L. M., Psychological Factors in Marital Happiness.
1 Tufts, J. H., America's Social Morality.

divorce is that couples marry too young." Recent investiga-
tions disclose that young people are prominent among those
seeking divorces.

Dr. Popenoe[1] declares that half the women in the United
States are married when they reach the age of twenty-two
and that the early twenties are the natural age at which
a girl should marry. Scientific studies[2] reveal that those
who marry before they reach twenty are unhappier than
those who marry later.

Dr. Groves[3] presents a wealth of statistical material concerning the ideal age of marriage. Evidence supports the
conviction that when either mate is nineteen or younger the
risk of achieving marital success is from ten to a hundred
times greater than when the groom is twenty-nine and the
bride of twenty-four. Four years on either of these age
standards make no appreciable difference.

One fact is clear: the odds are against both the man and
the girl who marry before they are twenty, and if they are
younger the likelihood of marital unhappiness increases in
proportion. Dr. Groves states that extremely youthful
marriages are especially hazardous: "It is apparent that in
our culture those who marry before they are twenty assume
the liabilities of inexperience, emotional immaturity, pre-
mature commitment. It is necessary, however, to recognize
that this is a cultural rather than a biological handicap." A
similar conclusion is reached by Himes in his excellent book
on marriage.

One may be fully developed physically yet be unprepared
for wedlock. It is important that he have a mental and
emotional background with personality factors that prepare

1 Popenoe, Paul, **Marriage, Before and After.**
2 Tufts, J. H., **America's Social Morality.**
3 Groves, Ernest R., **Marriage.**

him for a happy marriage. If an individual has grown up, according to Professor Terman, in a home where (1) the parents were happy, (2) he had a happy childhood, (3) there was absence of conflict with the mother and (4) the discipline in childhood was firm but not harsh, he is likely to be of a happy temperament and an all-around happy temperament is one of the greatest aids to a successful marriage.

If a girl has, unfortunately, been born into a home where parents wrangle and where discipline has been at the temper and convenience of a frustrated mother, she is likely to attempt marriage early to escape the home environment, but inevitably she will find in matrimony anything but satisfaction. A girl born and reared in a favorable home environment will be prepared for marriage much earlier in life than the former.

Another question relative to marriage is that of the difference in the ages of a man and wife. Since women arrive at womanhood earlier than a man reaches manhood, wives should, generally, be younger than their husbands. Where there is a great difference in age between husband and wife there is a tendency toward maladjustment. Each age has its peculiar tastes, aspirations, attractions, interests, hopes, pleasures and peculiarities. Even taste in entertainment changes. Music enjoyed by one may irritate the other. In order to live happily together a married couple should have common interests in as many fields of endeavor as possible.

When George Meredith was twenty he married a woman of thirty. It is evident from his **Modern Love** that he was unhappy in this relationship. If this congenial genius could not succeed in marriage with a woman his senior, it is doubtful if others could hope to find happiness in similar circumstances.

The average American husband is three years older than his wife. Studies of single women show that they want to marry a man who is from five to ten years their senior. Jung[1] believes that the bride should be two or three years younger than the groom, but thinks that when there is a difference of five years there is also a marked difference in interests, and ability to understand one who is half a decade or more younger. Dr. Terman found that maximum marital happiness was attained when the husband was from three to five years older than the bride. The next highest happiness score was achieved when the husbands were from four to ten years older than their wives. This and other studies reveal that the majority are most likely to find happiness when the age difference is not extreme. Age brings a different outlook on life. People tend to become more conservative with the years. A girl of eighteen will want to "go places," whereas the man of thirty will want to settle down and build a home. He will talk of saving money, and she will want to spend it.

The average girl who marries a man more than five years her senior will have additional adjustments to make, and the average man who marries a woman older than he will find that at the outset he has reduced the possibilities of his marital happiness. There are married couples in these what may be called "trying groups" that are extremely happy. Perhaps they would have been unhappy had they married in their own age group.

There is a type of temperament and emotional immaturity that proves the exception to the rule. This may be due

[1] Jung, Moses, **Modern Marriage.**

to algolagnic tendencies. The term "agolagnia" connotes the relationship between sexual excitement and pain. It is revealed in two forms: sadism and masochism. The sadist receives sex gratification from the experience of punishing or humiliating another person. The masochistic person experiences sexual emotion by receiving physical or mental subjugation. Regardless of age, when an active member and a passive member of the opposite sex meet, one offers the other the satisfaction he is seeking. Though their home may be a boisterous one, it would be shattered if either of them married a normal individual. Sadler has wisely called attention to the fact that "sadistic and masochistic proclivities are not always associated with sex gratification." He tells the story of a man nearly forty who repeatedly came to his wife with a paddle and insisted that she beat him soundly, much as his father did when he was a small boy. Three or four times a year he requested this spanking. Except for this peculiarity he appeared to be normal. Lest wives should think this a commendable practice, remember that only a sadistic wife would enjoy administering the punishment. The point is that a victim of algolagnic tendencies will, in all probability, find happiness in marriage if he marries one of an opposite type, regardless of age.

Some unconscious motives may be malicious and are, probably, the result of early childhood experiences. A woman may desire to dominate, and she marries a man younger than she. Perhaps because of a child-parent fixation a young man marries someone who reminds him of his mother and is much older than he. A woman may marry a man older than she to compensate for a father fixation. A man with a strong desire to be "mothered" will be happy with a motherly type of wife who is his senior.

Some of the conscious reasons why a young girl may marry an elderly man are these: pity for him in his lonely estate; a desire to be married and fear lest all opportunities be passed; purely mercenary motives. An older man is usually better able than a younger man to spend money on his bride.

It is conceivable that a normal person will select a mate who differs extremely in age and that both partners will live happily together. A marriage between those who differ widely in age may be transacted in good faith, but both partners will find that when one is separated from the other by a decade or more it is difficult to bridge the gap. Their friends, their interests and their purposes will drive a wedge between them which, with the passing of the years, will prohibit their becoming one. It appears that the more intelligent are more likely to bridge the gap, but in all probability the difference will be so great that the seeking and failure to find interests and intimate companionship will result in a persecution complex, a parent-child fixation or a platonic or undesirable friendship with another.

Those who were prompted by selfish interest to marry a much older or younger person have their reward, but that reward does not offer happiness. Any marriage prompted by a selfish motive offers nothing but the possibility of the fulfillment of that one desire. Such people live together, but never do "the twain" become "one flesh." Motives, no matter how well concealed, will, subjected to the strain of married life, reveal themselves. The older person will eventually detect the sincerity or insincerity that prompted a younger person to marry him or her. If the union is not founded upon love, the least that can happen is that esteem for the partner will die. Fichte said, "No true and enduring love can exist without esteem," and a marriage in which there is no love has failed.

WHAT DOES IT MEAN TO FALL IN LOVE?

CHAPTER 5

What Does It Mean to Fall in Love?

You may or may not "fall in love." You may come to love someone suddenly or gradually, depending upon your nature and temperament.

A girl writes, "I knew Bill in junior and senior high school. He was in a class ahead of mine. Bill was always nice to me, though I was younger than he. I never thought of him as a 'fellow', but as a good friend I could always depend upon to come to my aid when I needed an escort for a school function. We both graduated and went to different colleges. He invited me to his graduation and I went. This invitation was the first letter I had received from him, but we saw each other summers as we were neighbors. We were always friends but never thought of each other seriously. After the graduation exercises Bill said he would take me home if I had no one else in mind. We laughed about the way I use to call on him for emergencies in high school. Since that date I have seen him a number of times. I have fallen madly in love with him, and I want him more than anything else in the world. He loves me and wants to get married right away. Why this sudden change in both of us?"

In sharp contrast to this experience is that of a young man who grew up with a girl named Ann. They lived near each other, attended different schools, but were members of the same church and Sunday school. As children they were often together. The young man felt that "there was never a time that Ann and I did not love each other. We often told our parents about it but they laughed and said, 'You are just children. It is puppy love.' Maybe they were right, but whatever it was it has not changed. We both gave each other the opportunity to date others, but no one else came into our lives who interested us. I think we have given ourselves a fair chance to discover if we are truly in love. We want to be happy. To our minds our future happiness rests in our marrying. Do you think we should have wider acquaintances first?" They married without being able to designate any day as the date they fell in love, and yet their love is as genuine as the first couple's.

These young people had this in common: they both knew the partners they married. They had grown to love one whom they had known for a long time. This is the way love works. It is a growth rather than a fall.

The young lady who learned to love Bill did not fall in love suddenly, as she thought. It has been said that "it's safe enough to fall in love if one is careful when he falls." But such action requires efforts, control and planning. More that emotion is involved; the mind directs the course of action.

Each of these young people established, through experience and knowledge, a standard for his or her life-partner. As they matured, judgment developed. The qualities which they desired in their partners they found in one they already knew. The first girl discovered the fact suddenly. Why? When she reached the age at which she could consider marriage, she found in Bill the type of man that she should marry. Perhaps her early and happy association with him had caused her, unconsciously, to make him her ideal as a husband. Seeing him again caused her to associate all the happiness of youth with the pattern of her ideal-Bill.

The young man who married the girl whom he had met in childhood did not experience a sudden emotional upheaval when he declared his love to her, yet his love was as genuine as if it had been accompanied by an emotional disturbance. Ann proved to be a congenial companion. He saw her frequently enough to realize that she added to his enjoyment of life. He had grown to associate her with pleasantness and happiness. Time had convinced him of her worth.

A man who falls in love with a girl is usually attracted to her. There is something about her that catches his eye. He expresses a desire to meet her. Often the meeting suffices. Occasionally it leads to months or years of courtship or it may result in a speedy marriage. The hasty marriage is justified on the ground that it is "love at first sight." This is an unsound hypothesis by which to justify unwarranted haste. Dr. Groves has observed that "a marriage choice is not predominantly concerned with qualities or with possessions, but with personality." Personality is not discovered easily or quickly. It unfolds itself to one who can patiently comprehend its meaning and ways. A hasty marriage is in danger of being governed by physical attraction rather than by spiritual qualities. It is fashioned on something that is a part of the individual, but not the individual. Such a sudden "falling in love" may not be love, but merely fascination.

That which first attracts one individual to another may be mental or physical stimuli based on beauty or proficiency, but this attraction must be supported by love if it is to develop. Sex appeal is an important factor in marriage, but it is not love. A man with low moral standards may seek a woman who has sex appeal but he has little regard or concern for her. The girl with talent may attract a desirable companion, but though he respects her ability, unless love develops there can be no enduring happiness in a marriage between two such partners.

Not all "first attractions" lead to genuine love, nor do they lead to unhappy marriages. The outcome depends upon one's preparation for love.

The normal girl dreams of love. She anticipates the day when she will fall in love with a handsome man, marry, be loved and have her own home. This aspiration is normal and should be encouraged: It is dangerous only when it is not properly directed by reason. Modern movies and much current literature have presented love as something which sweeps a girl off her feet and compels her to do she knows not what or why. Today's conception of love pictures rich men renouncing fortunes, deserting families, shunning society and being ostracized for love. It presents a man who meets a girl and marries her the same day. This is a false

1 Cabot, Richard, **What Men Live By**

conception of true marital love. Dr. Cabot[1] has well advised that "we must free the word 'love' from its association with boudoirs and morbid novels and try to identify it with something genuine and all-purposive, to ally it with the great sane forces of nature."

Literature that appeals to the animal forces of nature does not engender love but baseness. Tolstoy was correct in saying that "lawless act stirs up lawless love." It is restrained love, like that which Dante had for Beatrice, which makes a person capable of enduring love.

There is an appeal that is purely sexual, but men do not marry the girl who has nothing else to offer. Men marry the girl who offers love that is pure and discriminating. Groves reveals that "it is axiomatic that however strongly individuals are attracted to each other by sex appeal, they seldom desire to marry and never do so safely unless they share, in large measure, similar social background."

In an effort to call attention to the importance of sex in marriage, some writers have overemphasized the subject. This overemphasis has caused some, especially young women, to worry unduly and ask, "Will I be capable of sex passion?" rather than to inquire of themselves, "Am I capable of true and devout love?" Other people have confused passion with love, and because they experience emotional reactions to a suitor, they think they have discovered love.

Allurement is sometimes mistaken for love. A girl who anticipates love but who has had no ardent suitor may suddenly find herself worshiped by a charming young man. Her response may be "I have fallen in love." She has been awakened by a new experience which arouses her anticipated emotional reaction. The new experience of receiving

attention from and "caring for" someone will give thrill and
allurement to her fancy. This is not love but emotional
excitement. The wise action is to wait. "Love suffereth
long, and is kind." Impatience, especially if it is accompanied by unkindness due to delay, signifies lack of love. The
waiting period should add to the fervor of love rather than
weaken it. Any man who cannot wait a few months to prove
his love to a girl has no right to ask her on short acquaintance to spend the rest of her life with him. The impatience
bespeaks his lack of stability and his inability to face
successfully the long years of marriage.

As has been suggested, the subconscious mind plays a
prominent place in "love at first sight." Your subconscious
may attempt to end your quest for a life-partner by sug-
gesting that the first person who shows serious interest in
you is the proper partner. Fear also plays a large part,
though they may not be aware of it, in the reactions of some
women. Fear says, "This may be your last chance at love."
Naturally, rationalization begins. One sees in the person
concerned the qualities desired in a companion. The most
unreasonable excuses are offered to defend any apparent
weakness.

A person may fall in love with a member of the opposite
sex who meets certain physical requirements. For example,
a girl may like curly red hair. One day she meets a young
man who meets her specifications, and she falls violently
in love with him, but in reality his only qualification may be
purely physical: his red curls. If the girl should marry him,
she may or may not be happy. The possibility of happiness
will be dependent upon spiritual qualities which the young
man may possess. "If you marry for anything but love, you
marry for what may perish in a night." There must be

something spiritual about the youth, something substantial that the girl can admire, if she is to marry for love.

If you are the type of girl who has talked much about marriage, you may be one who indulges in romantic excitement. You may be in love with love. If that be true, you are in danger of marrying for love of love. These fires are quickly kindled but soon subside unless there is something behind your love to feed the flames. The flame may die and leave you neither love nor the attraction to be loved. Should this occur, you will be like a half-burned log in a fireplace, neither attractive nor comforting.

Family relation fixations sometime prompt "love at first sight." Consider one example. A girl was deeply devoted to her only brother. When he married she was heartbroken. She developed a strong hatred for his wife because she had "stolen" her brother from her. The girl was miserable until she met a young man who resembled her brother in physical appearance and manner. She was ready to marry him the moment she saw him, and he lost little time in proposing. Fortunately the groom possessed a fine character and was an excellent husband. He did not realize that the girl did not love him, but her own brother. Eventually the bride made a happy transference of affection from her brother to her husband, and her abnormal state of fixation found a desirable outlet in her marriage. Marital happiness was saved by the fact that the young man was a Christian and possessed Christian qualities which are the same always, regardless of the person who possesses them.

A man or woman's home training, the attitude of parents toward each other, emotional and mental stability and experiences all determine his or her response to love and the ability to distinguish it from fascination and passion.

Love is foundational in marriage. A marriage cannot weather the storms and rains of changing seasons unless it is built upon this sure foundation. "The most wonderful thing in the world," wrote Dorsey,[1] "is love — love of man for woman, love of woman for man; nothing else can be so lovable, nothing else can be so perfect. No other relationship can be so beautifully, normally, naturally and eternally complete. It is of all human institutions the most ancient and the most honorable; it is the keystone of human families, which are the pillars of society."

It is this "most wonderful thing in the world" that people seek in marriage. It is an irresistible force. What lies behind it? What is it that a partner seeks in love?

There are certain qualities that attract people to each other. Some of these interests are prompted by the unconscious. We like certain people because we have had happy associations in childhood with someone whom they resemble. Pleasant past memories cause one to feel kindly toward him. We like him instinctively.

There are other people to whom we are consciously attracted because of their decorum, personal appearance, good taste, neatness, charm or physical appeal. The attraction may lead to admiration, and admiration is akin to love. Admiration is not love but there can be no love without it.

The characteristics that cause one person to admire another may not be detected by others. You may hear one person say of another, "I can't see what she sees to admire in him." But the fact is that the admirer sees something he thinks is worthy of admiration. Indeed, the one who offers the criticism may see fine traits in the person but because of jealousy will not acknowledge them.

[1] Dorsey, George A., **How and Why's of Human Behavior.**

Respect is another attribute that is akin to love, but it is not love. Love, nevertheless, cannot live where it is not found. Once a man loses respect for his wife he can no longer love her, and the same is true of a woman's attitude toward a husband. Admiration, respect and love are a necessary trinity for a happy married life. One is dependent upon the other. When one is lost, the other two soon depart.

The first step in falling in love is attraction. Some purpose or motive attracts you to the other person. To marry for attraction is not like marrying for love. Attraction should lead to admiration, and admiration should prompt love. Admiration is a part of love. "We need must love the highest." Only pure motives can call forth pure love, which leads to a union in whch two become as one.

The goal which love seeks in marriage is the blending of two lives into one, so that the identity of one is virtually lost. Rawlins[1] says, "You identify yourself with your beloved when you fall in love; you put yourself in his place; and all his problems become your problems, just as though the two of you had become one."

Jesus stated that in the beginning God made man and woman, and said, "For this cause shall a man leave father and mother, and shall cleave to his wife: and they twain shall be one flesh. Wherefore they are no more twain, but one flesh. What therefore God hath joined together, let not man put asunder." Jesus emphasizes the unity of marriage. Those whom God has joined together are one. He further states that this was part of the divine plan from the beginning. The union of man and wife in wedlock is the unfinished work of creation. Marriage, founded on love, makes man a creator with God.

1 Rawlins, Robert A., **Success in Love and Marriage.**

In the beginning God made man and woman. Then God rested. Creation was to continue as man and woman became creators. Animal instincts were not to bring them together, for they were conscious beings. They were to be united by love. God is love. Love united the first man and woman in marriage, or to state the truth in another way, God joined them in holy wedlock. In a love-motivated marriage, the unfinished work of the Creator finds its consummation in God, man and woman. When we see a Christian renounce friends and fortune, relatives and kin to marry a person he loves, we may be witnessing the power of unfinished creation working in his life.

A true marriage, then, should end division and strife and lead to a unity of spirit and purpose, as a divine plan undergirds married life.

It is natural that there should be differences of opinion and opposing views on various subjects, but these variations do not disturb the harmony of the love life of the two.

Other men and other women may become the couple's good friends, but the married lovers have allegiance and fidelity to only one person. That person has a unique and holy relationship which no one else can assume as long as his partner lives. There is something in the relationship of a man and wife, brought together by love, that gives them a feeling of oneness so that either can say, "We are one." This oneness does not restrict but enriches the life of the other. They have a unity and purpose in life for which Jesus prayed: ". . . that they may be one, as we are."

It is this unconscious desire to complete their lives that causes people to fall in love. Plato taught this conception of love. He stated that love was the entering of the divorced half of the original human being into union with its counterpart.

There is one more question that needs to be answered: Does true love run smooth? The answer is: Yes, if you give it sufficient time. In the beginning, true love may be the cause of much unrest and quarreling. A lover may discontinue his courtship, but it will be disrupted only for a short time if his love is genuine. The reason for this is all a part of the purpose of true love.

Paul, speaking with profound insight, said that "love envieth not." This remark appears, at first, superfluous. How could there be a relationship between envy and love? This is like saying that snow is not black. But Paul did not waste words and was careful in his choice of them. By this statement he wanted to convey a truth.

Paul holds the key to the question "What is love?" We are not to be envious of the one whom we truly love. It is not uncommon to see a man who is envious of a woman's ability fall suddenly in love with her. Lover's quarrels during courtship occur among the most devoted. It is evident that envy and growing love may operate in close relationship. When love is genuine and lasting, envy is crowded out.

Envy is usually the result of fear, and the cure for fear is love. "Perfect love casteth out fear." A man can never truly love a woman who gives him cause for fear. This is why fidelity is paramount in love. **Advice to a Lover,** by William Cobbett, is pertinent at this point. He writes, "A loose woman is a disagreeable acquaintance: what must she be, then, as a wife? Love is so blind, and vanity is so busy in persuading us that our own qualities will be sufficient to ensure fidelity, that we are very apt to think nothing, or, at any rate, very little, of trifling symptoms of levity; but if such symptoms show themselves now, we may be well assured that we shall never possess the power of effecting a cure. Your 'free and hearty' girls I have liked very well to talk and laugh with, but never, for one moment, did it enter into my mind that I could have endured a 'free and hearty' girl for a wife. Gross indeed is the beast, for he is unworthy the name of man, nasty indeed is the wretch, who can even entertain a thought of putting himself between a pair of sheets with a wife of whose infidelity he possesses the proof; but in such cases a man ought to be very slow to believe appearances, and he ought not to decide against his wife but upon the clearest proof. The last and, indeed, the only effectual safeguard is to begin well, to make a good choice, to let the beginning be such as to render infidelity and jealousy next to impossible. If you begin in grossness, if you couple yourself on to one with whom you have taken liberties, infidelity is the natural and just consequence."

As long as either partner lacks confidence in the other, there cannot be a pure and satisfying love. There will be jealousy and where there is jealousy, love has not reached fulfillment.

Envy may be present for another purpose: an individual may see qualities in his beloved which he wants to possess himself. It may be that he has a quick temper, and the girl he admires is calm and poised. When a situation arises that troubles him, she keeps calm. He envies and at the same time admires such an attitude. He wishes he had such composure. In her he sees the person he wants to be. If he is a decided egotist, he may eventually criticize the girl rather than admire her, or he may unconsciously envy her ability and seek it for himself by making her his wife.

Plato entertained the thought that lovers seek a likeness in each other. Adler contended that couples "are mutually attracted to each other and their fellowship is an expression of their desires and need of each other." Love requires a common interest, but one person may possess a trait which the other does not have and desires. The difference is not one of attitude, interest or purpose, but of temperamental or emotional ability.

When confronted with responsibilities a person may become conscious of weakness in his life. These defects may drive him into a depressed mental state or cause him to seek help from one in whom he can confide. The latter course is the normal one. The man may begin to tell his troubles to a girl he admires or unconsciously envies because she possesses the talent or stability which he feels he lacks. If her response is congenial and helpful, he will become more closely attracted and attached to her. Envy or love may follow, depending largely upon her sympathetic attitude.

The girl who listens attentively to the young man faced with responsibility and difficulty will either draw him to her or drive him away, depending upon her ability to furnish what he needs to fortify his life. If he finds that she lacks the quality he seeks, he will search for another who can furnish what he needs.

Theodore Reik,[1] in a book that every young lover should read, and which I cannot commend too highly, makes the observation that a person who "falls in love" has an ego ideal which he exchanges for an individual in whom are to be found the qualities that he desires for himself. This is the

1 A Psychologist Looks on Love.

point which I wish to emphasize. The youth does not fall in love with "brains" or "talent"; he falls in love with a personality who possesses what he lacks. That brings us again to the story of creation which tells us that God said, "It is not good that the man should be alone. I will make him an help meet for him." The quest for that helpmeet is the search for love.

One falls in love because he recognizes his imperfection and desires to correct it. Recognizing in another what he lacks may at first produce envy, but desiring to perfect himself, he continues his quest. He may experience unrest and a feeling of defeat that makes him disagreeable at home. Wise parents will excuse his actions on the ground that "he is in love." In reality he wants to be in love. When he finds a member of the opposite sex who possesses a similar attitude and purpose, one who is a companion and a friend, he falls in love with and eventually marries her. Her ability and composure will increase his own feeling of inferiority thus making his restlessness more acute. Envy and love may intermingle for a time until love triumphs.

It is exceedingly important that the girl possess the quality or qualities that he needs. She may lack other important characteristics but as long as she is companionable and excels where he is difficult she is his ideal. Having found what he needs for happiness, he has found the right wife.

A man falls in love with a woman who supplements his life. He is not himself without her. Only with her can his life be complete. She possesses the quality he seeks in his own life, and he makes that quality his own by marrying her. The two become as one because she becomes so completely a part of him that her assets are his. He acquired this through love and marriage. He married her to make his life a unity. In such a fortunate union the man's basic desires are fulfilled. He is guaranteed affection, love security and significance. He has found a woman who loves him, who possesses the qualities he needs, and he now feels he can make a contribution to society. He has fulfilled what his basic urges demand for a satisfied and well-balanced married life.

MIXED MARRIAGES AND HAPPINESS

CHAPTER 6

Mixed Marriages and Happiness

It is to insure their future happiness that two people contract to enter into marriage. They are certain that their love for each other will surmount any obstacle. Perhaps they are right, but mixed marriages place before them one of the most troublesome obstacles they will encounter. Many who are thus united do not anticipate the problems that lie ahead. This chapter aims to call attention to some of the serious difficulties that arise from mixed marriages. These perplexities are real and must be given serious and careful attention. Many young people, entering into marriage without realizing what is involved, say when disaster threatens them, "We never knew so many difficulties could arise." Youth should be acquainted with the numerous problems introduced into life by mixed marriages. With a full knowledge of the situation, let a young man or woman make the choice. It is the duty of older people to state the problem. It is the task of youth to make a sane decision.

The types of mixed marriages that will be discussed in this chapter are the marriage of Christians to non-believers, of Protestants to Catholics or Jews, of Americans to foreigners, those of foreign extraction or interracial groups, and of single persons to those who have been married.

1. Can a Christian be happily married to a non-believer? If one is a careless church member and the other is indifferent to the Church, they will eventually become unbelievers or lukewarm in their attitude toward Christianity. They will probably rear their family in such an atmosphere. They must contend also with the fact that non-religious people as a whole encounter more unhappiness in marriage than those to whom religion is important.

If an active Christian marries an unbeliever, problems will inevitably arise. Not a few married men and women live under such conditions. One attends divine services while the other sleeps. Fellowship in the Church, centered around groups of married couples, leaves the unfortunate partner alone. The unbeliever does not want to support the Church and may forbid it. He may laugh at his mate's faith and scoff at things held sacred by her. There are no united family devotions or prayers in time of trouble. If religion and the Church mean much to one and nothing to the other, there is a diversity of interest concerning a pertinent and vital subject. The zealous Christian is concerned about his partner's attitude, and this concern irritates him.

The question of amusements and entertainment also presents a problem. The Lord's Day is honored by the Christian whereas the nonbeliever goes fishing or attends a Sunday movie. One may go to church on Sunday while the other goes to a poolroom, a bowling alley or stays in bed and listens to the radio. On weekdays the same problem becomes more acute. Different attitudes toward entertainment or recreation may cause quarreling. One may delight in attending a Sunday school social; the other may frequent a beer parlor. The advice of Paul is timely: "Be ye not unequally yoked together with unbelievers: for what fellowship hath righteousness with unrighteousness? . . . or what part hath he that believeth with an infidel? And what agreement hath the temple of God with idols? for ye are the temple of the living God."

The admonition to Christians not to identify themselves with unbelievers is not based on prejudice but is offered in the interest of mankind. Lack of fellowship, unity and harmony is inevitable in such a union.

A Christian and a non-Christian are bound to have different views of marriage. The approach of the first will be colored by his fidelity to God; the other will lack this deep spiritual reverence. "The real reason for many marriages ending disastrously," says Dr. Coutts,[1] "is that man and wife have not even tried the Christian way . . . men who regard marriage as a sacrament of the Church can never find common ground with those who think of marriage as being, at its best, a mere social utility, and at its worst an intolerant bondage."

1 Coutts, John W., **The Church and the Sex Question.**

If men and women need Christianity to increase their
marital happiness they must, at least, know what Christianity teaches and requires of the devotee. The studies of
Dr. Fiske[1] show that Christians find help from their faith
in solving their marital problems. He writes, "A Christian
home has seven times the chance of being permanent and
unbroken as the irreligious home has . . . the Christian
religion is our best possible insurance against divorce." He
quotes a judge who has had long experience on the bench
as saying that he had never divorced two persons who were
both members of the same church. Dr. Fiske states that
less than 2 percent of church-attending white families in
America, and perhaps 1 percent of communicant families,
are even divorced. One of the reasons he offers for this
is that "the whole Christian movement has always opposed
self-indulgence, which is a major symptom in the disease of
selfishness and the chief cause of the troubles leading to
divorce." More recent research[2] supports the findings of
Dr. Fiske.

A Christian should determine his attitude toward an
un-believer in the early days of courtship. To marry with
the hope that the non-Christian may be changed after
marriage is not wise. What one will not do before marriage
to fulfill the expectations of his espoused he seldom does
afterward. Paul advised Christians who are already married
to non-Christians to live with them and try to turn them to
Christ. "Let not the wife depart from her husband: but and
if she depart, let her remain unmarried, or be reconciled to
her husband: and let not the husband put away his wife . . .
If any brother hath a wife that believeth not, and she is

[1] Fiske, George W., The Christian Family.
[2] Burgess, Ernest W., and Cottrell, Leonard S., Jr., Predicting Success or Failure in
Marriage.

pleased to dwell with him, let him not put her away. And
the woman which hath an husband that believeth not, and
if he be pleased to dwell with her, let her not leave him . . .
For what knowest thou, O wife, whether thou shalt save thy
husband? or how knowest thou, O man, whether thou shalt
save thy wife?"

The wedding of a Christian to a non-Christian is fraught
with complex implications that should be faced seriously
before the courtship has progressed far. Which choice
will you make before you enter into "an honorable institution ordained of God"? You cannot ignore the question
or hope for the best. The choice you make will determine
not only your own happiness but that of your children.
Major Christian denominations advise against the marriage
of a believer to a non-believer on the ground that unless
the Christian possesses rare virtue "the strain of attempted
adjustments will be found to be too severe for any good
and happy solution to their common problem."

2. **Protestants, Catholics and Jews alike do not favor
mixed marriages.** The Catholic Church not only advises
Catholics against marrying non-Catholics but makes rigid
demands upon the non -Catholic. He must have been baptized
and produce a certification of baptism. He may be married
only by a Catholic priest. The Catholic who marries a non-
Catholic is denied certain privileges and blessings. The
non-Catholic must pledge that he will not restrict the size
of his family and that his children will be reared as Catholics,
even should the Catholic partner die. He must agree further
to interfere in no manner with the faith of the Catholic
partner, although the Catholic may and should interfere
with his faith.

When a Catholic marries a non-Catholic, the couple is

governed from the outset by the authority of one church. This does not lead to happiness. Rather, it causes one to be subordinate to the wishes of the other in the bearing and rearing of children. The Catholic Church clearly states its position and Protestants who consider marrying Catholics should be familiar with the demands of the Church: "With the Protestant, any church but the Catholic is good enough. With the Catholic, Christ established one Church, not a series of discordant churches, and that Church is Catholic . . . For your happiness and the happiness of the children God may give you, marry your own."[1] Canon law provides that the Catholic spouse should endeavor to convert the non-Catholic: "The Church may never permit Catholics to marry those of other religious professions except under the two-fold condition that the Catholic party will be undisturbed in the free exercise of his or her religion and that all the offspring be brought up in Catholicism."[2]

In the marriage of a Catholic to a non-Catholic or "one belonging to a schism or heresy the Church reluctantly consents to the union, and the ritual withholds her blessing, says no mass, and does not permit the marriage to be solemnized in the Church." In addition to this, bans are not published and the ring is not blessed.

If one has deep-seated religious convictions he cannot regard this rule lightly. Demands imposed upon him by a church, or as Catholics teach, "The Church," are likely to antagonize him. He may be willing to be married in a parish house, but a girl who has planned, with her parents, a church wedding, begins her marriage with a disappointment. The sense of religious inferiority imposed upon the non-Catholic does not favor a happy attitude at the time of marriage.

1 Lord, David A., S. J., *Marry Your Own.*
2 Lonergan, Wm. L., *Mixed Marriages — A Catholic View.*

Dr. Popenoe contends that "it is a great handicap when persons who have been brought up in unlike religious faiths marry. It cannot be said that they will fail to be happy, but there is risk of this finally resulting if they do not have from the beginning an appreciation of their differences and some acceptable program in regard to this, particularly if they should have children. Great separation in the religious point of view easily leads to unusual strain." Some of the causes for an "unusual strain" in Protestant-Catholic marriages are the following.

a.   **The difference in religious background causes difficulty.** One's faith is established in childhood. It grows out of parental instruction and early participation in divine services and ritual. Similarity of early emotional expression in religion encourages happiness in marriage. One's religious background becomes a part of the texture and fiber of his life. He may think he can ignore this potent factor in marital happiness but it is rooted in the subconscious. When married life brings its responsibilities, a troubled soul will inevitably return to a childhood faith which gave him comfort and assurance. At a time when two people need unity of faith to hold their distressed lives together, a mixed marriage prevents them from finding it.

A man married a Catholic girl and united with her church so that she could have a church wedding. He took this action to please her but displeased his parents. All went well until his wife became conscious of the fact that he was not fulfilling his obligations to the Catholic Church. Her distress was further increased when he expressed a desire to send their son to a Protestant Sunday school, where the child could learn the Bible and "recite pieces on

Children's Day with the other children." The family began
to quarrel and finally separated.

b.   **Conflicting religious views of parents, in-laws, relatives and friends place a strain upon the couple's fellowship
with them.** For example, a Protestant wife may invite her
husband's family to a steak dinner on Friday or innocently
ignore Holy Day regulations and restrictions imposed upon
devotees by the church.

Conversation of an intimate nature will need to be
guarded. The non-Catholic must be warned lest he make
foolish remarks about that which to him is not sacred but
which to the Catholic is holy and supreme.

In a happy marriage the bride's and the groom's parents
should co-operate to make the newly-married couple feel
accepted. Parents who have embraced the Protestant faith
all their lives cannot feel perfectly happy in the home of a
daughter-in-law who has taken their son away from or
made him indifferent to their faith. The same will be true of
Catholic parents under similar circumstances.

c.   **The difficulty of discharging religious responsibilities
and receiving the ministry of the Church becomes involved.**
Which church will you support financially? What religious
holy days will you observe? If there is sickness in the
house, will you call both the priest and the pastor? Will you
compromise in your faith and unite with one church, and if
so, can you do it wholeheartedly? These are some of the
issues which must be faced.

d.   **The place that religion should have in the home is
bound to be dominated by one of the partners.** The Catholic
cannot participate in a non-Catholic service. It is for him
a sin to do so, and such an action requires confession and

penitence. The Protestant must make no attempt to interfere with the religion of the Catholic. This means that the Catholic religious journals, which often denounce Protestants, must be permitted in the home if the Catholic desires them. The Protestant will need to exercise extreme caution in the type of religious journals he leaves on the library table lest they denounce the faith of his partner.

The mixed marriage divides a family on the one day above all on which it should be united — Sunday. Children in such homes can go to church with either parent, but not both.

3. **The marriages of Protestants to Jews are not so numerous as Catholic-Protestant unions.** One contemplating a Protestant-Jewish union, however, should recognize that Judaism is more than a religion. It is a culture. The details of Jewish ritual, dietary rules and holidays demand attention. Judaism rejects Christ as the Messiah, and consequently there is no Christian Christmas for Jews. The New Year is celebrated on a different date, as are many other holy days. Easter is the Christian's day of triumph, but it can have no such meaning for the Jews. All this, with the problems presented by Catholic-Protestant marriages, emphasizes the undesirability of intermarriage between Christians and Jews.

4. **International and interracial marriages are exceedingly difficult to preserve.** In these unions the divorce rate is high and unhappiness is common. There are greater possibilities for happiness when an American marries one born in America of foreign parentage than if he should marry the same girl had she been born in another country. The American born of foreign parents is familiar with the traditions, customs and political life of America. Were the same girl to be born and reared in a foreign country

she would be indoctrinated with the traditions and peculiarities of her national life.

5.   **When Americans marry those from foreign countries, there are different customs, cultural standards, attitudes toward members of the opposite sex, views regarding authority in the home, codes of morality and basic philosophies of life to separate them.**

6.   **In racial groups there are certain established customs that are deeply engrained in one's nature.** There is also difficulty in finding mutual friends and social standing for one's self or his family. A white person may marry a Negro in the North and upon moving to the South find that the state laws prohibit the marriage of Negroes to white persons. There are also laws in certain states prohibiting the marriage of white people to Chinese and Japanese. These facts indicate the difficulties that await those who marry into foreign and interracial groups.

One of the serious obstacles to happiness in interracial marriages is the American's feeling of superiority. This attitude was evident in Europe and Asia during World War II. Thousands of Americans married girls in other lands — girls who listened with eyes aglow to the tales told them by servicemen about the land of milk and honey: America. The least one can wish for the brides now coming to America is that they will be happier than the 10,000 French brides who married Americans during World War I. Of those marriages 8,000 ended in divorce. Two people with unusual patience, charity and love are required to make an interracial marriage a success. Research reveals the hazards of interracial marriages.

7.   **Another type of mixed marriage is that of a single person to one who has been married.** This includes those

whose marriages have been dissolved by annulment, death or divorce. An annulment is not a divorce. The court rules that when annulment occurs, the marriage never existed. The license for such a marriage was obtained through fraud or was illegally contracted, and fraud invalidates marriage. The girl uses her maiden name, but she cannot escape the reality that she assumed the obligations involved in marriage and can never be free from the fact that she was a wife. She may plead inexperience or ignorance in entering into the contract, but one who is seeking a divorce may make a similar assertion. An annulment, unlike a divorce, is granted to a couple who never attempted to live together over a long period as man and wife. The criticism against them is not that they failed in marriage but that they failed to sense or appreciate what marriage involved. This may not be true of both partners, but the transaction shows lack of discernment.

A discussion of this type of mixed marriage includes the person who was married before but whose partner died. Before falling in love with one who was married previously, the single person should realize that such a union may be desirable, but there are pertinent facts to consider before taking wedding vows.

Know all you can about the married life of your prospective mate. At what age was the first marriage contracted? Was it a happy union, and if so, why? If not, who was at fault?

One needs to know the attitude of the prospective mate toward his first spouse. Do you remind him of her? If so, is that the reason you were chosen? It is dangerous to marry someone because you remind him of a former lover. Ask yourself these questions: "Why do I want a spouse

who has been married? Do I realize that I may be jealous
of one who is dead?" The person who was happily married
is likely to refer to his departed partner on many occasions.
If one has a jealous nature, there will be an excuse for envy.

If there were children from the previous marriage you
will be called upon to fill the roll of stepparent. This is a
responsibility which demands a careful consideration and
Christian character.

A married couple will have associations with certain
people. The living partner, if happy in his first marriage,
will want to retain those ties. Friends which you have not
chosen will be in the family circle. Can you accept this
"ready-made" setting?

After one has weighed all these facts he should realize
that to marry one who has been married before cannot be
the same as to marry one not previously married. There is
not the element of new adventure which characterizes a
marriage between two single people. You cannot share
certain intimate experiences. The honeymoon will not mean
the same to both of you, and you will not begin married life
and home-building in the same manner.

After one has taken into consideration the differences
involved and has assured himself that no ulterior motive
prompts the union, he may be exceedingly happy in being
married to one who has acquired experience and understanding through a marriage dissolved in death. Men are not
so willing to marry a woman who has been previously
married as are women to marry men who have had wives.
The question becomes chiefly one involving women. They
must decide if they are prompted by love to marry one who
once loved and lost through death and desires to love again.

Divorce presents a different problem and is exceedingly

precarious because much is involved. Is one justified in taking a vow to cleave to another "until death do us part" and then dissolve that marriage in court? The majority of American women agree, according to research, that divorce should be permitted, that uniform laws should regulate it and that women should not marry with the mental reservation that divorce can free them. But to agree to the first permits the latter.

Christ taught that the only possible ground for divorce was connubial infidelity, because it wholly subverted the marriage vows. But He said also that even those separated were not to remarry, though they were innocent of offense.

Divorce crept into society after James I declared that a women who had not heard from her husband for a series of years could assume that he was dead and remarry. On the basis of this law the colonists began to legislate added causes for separation. At present it is not difficult to get a divorce. In fact, the couple may agree to separate, and one partner may charge another with mental cruelty or incompatibility and the other may not contest the case. Divorce will then follow swiftly.

Pope Leo III wisely foresaw that "divorce once being tolerated there would be no restraint powerful enough to keep it within the limits fixed or foreseen."

The Catholic Church and some Protestant bodies will not recognize the marriage of a divorced person. Sociologists condemn divorce because of the harm it brings to society. "History shows that monogamy has always been accompanied by increasing vigor in the society or group practicing it, and its opposite—freedom from social restraint, in the relationship of men and women, has always been associated

with social or group decay."[1] Psychologists condemn divorce
on the basis that it solves nothing. "Matrimony is a
venerable institution, not a continuous state of bliss. The
great fallacy of divorce is that it predicts a change of
partners as beneficial. But marriage does not change."[2]

The divorce rate in America has steadily increased. There
was a 40-percent increase following World War I, and the
outlook following World War II is discouraging. One
American marriage in every five now ends in divorce, with
one divorce for every two marriages in certain areas which
is the rate predicted for the nation in 1960. Divorce not only
breaks the heart of a mate but forces children to grow up
without the much-needed guidance of a happy home. In
the 20,000 divorces pending in America the welfare of more
than 50,000 children is involved.

The chief causes of divorce are: mothers-in-law, hasty
marriage, lax divorce laws, poor preparation for marriage,
unfavorable home environment, lack of religion and excessive drunkenness.

Statistics declare that mothers-in-law are a chief cause
of divorce. The mother-in-law is not necessarily malicious,
but she is jealous of the attention and affection which her
child shows to her husband. Her fault-finding and criticism
cause dissatisfaction that may result in divorce.

The year 1945 saw an all-time high in divorce in the
city of Philadelphia when 5,286 divorce suits were filed and
3,475 decrees granted. The outcome for 1946 is even more
distressing. In the first five months of the year, 9,131
marriage licenses were issued and 3,237 divorce suits
brought. For the week of June 22, 533 marriage licenses
were granted and 236 divorce decrees given.[1]

1 Groves, Ernest R. and Gladys H., **Good Housekeeping,** August, 1938.
2 Jung, Karl, **Cosmopolitan,** July, 1937.

Judge Corrale, of Common Pleas Court No. 2 of Philadelphia, states that lack of religion is the major factor in divorce. He says of divorce, "I blame it primarily to a lack of religion." Judge Lewis of the same court states, "Overindulgence in alcoholic beverages we find to be a cause of disagreement in a large percentage of the divorce cases we hear."

Judge Christensen, of the Municipal Court of Beloit, Wisconsin, states that "drinking in taverns is a factor in more than 90 per cent of our divorce cases." Leslie Weatherhead,[2] who contends that the ideal to be upheld is that nothing should break the marriage bond, regardless of circumstances, agrees that "every actual divorce does something to lessen the status of marriage in the mind of the community and to shake its faith in the wedded state. Those who look on, and especially the children of divorced parents, can never see marriage with the bloom on it. Their vision is spoiled by the divorce of people near them."

One interesting fact discovered by psychologists is that divorced women were more unstable emotionally and less interested in humanitarian enterprises than happily married women. The divorcées preferred sophisticated reading material above the Bible or religious literature. Students who pursue courses in family and marital relationships have lower divorce rates than those who follow no such plan. Religion and preparation for marriage are, therefore, lacking in the lives of the majority who seek divorces.

How can the divorce rate be reduced? By making America a Christian nation, by properly preparing those who are about to marry, and by publishing the true facts and results of divorce. Dr. Popenoe says that "the majority of divorces

1 Don Fairbanks, **The Evening Bulletin**, Philadelphia, **Saturday, June 29, 1946.**
2 **The Mastery of Sex.**

are not only unnecessary but undesirable, and in many
instances both husband and wife are worse off after
terminating the marriage than before . . . many of the
divorcees find the readjustment not only difficult but impossible: so the death rate, the suicide rate, the insanity
rate and the rate of commitment to prison are two or three
times as high for divorcees as they are for married people
of the same age."

A marriage to a divorced person is a stamp of approval
upon divorce. When it becomes difficult, by law, through the
Church, and as a result of the attitude assumed by those
eligible to marry, for the divorcee to remarry, there will
be fewer divorces.

Marriage is more than a legal contract. It is a divinely
appointed joining together of man and woman by God. God
alone can annul the agreement. He is counselor, not man.
I am reminded in this connection of a woman who for
sixty years anticipated the return of the man who left her
after less than two years of married life. Many men sought
her company, but she refused their overtures and toiled
and prayed and hoped. Her dreams never came true. Had
she remarried she would undoubtedly have had a happy
home, but there are many happy homes today because girls
now married who knew her have followed her pattern of
fidelity.

THE ENGAGEMENT PERIOD

CHAPTER 7

The Engagement Period

The engagement period is more intimate and more substantial than the days of courtship, but less familiar and assuring than marriage. It is adorned with happiness and satisfaction, yet at the same time is fraught with dissatisfaction and restlessness. Although it ends many worries it creates new perplexities.

To realize at the beginning that periods of doubt, fear and discontent accompany the engagement is to be prepared to deal with such adversities rationally. The new relationship of the engagement period will place a strain on both parties, a strain which demands mutual understanding and sympathy.

A couple should know each other intimately before they become engaged. A satisfactory courtship should develop naturally into an engagement. During the time that the young people keep company the man will make known his desire to marry. Most proposals do not come as a surprise to the girl. In the course of courting the desire to wed is made known.

It is enlightening to read how famous persons proposed. There was an easiness about the act that made it far from austere and lifeless. The proposals were individualistic.

Every man will offer his proposal in a different manner, depending upon the length of his courtship and the subjects discussed freely during it.

It is considered common courtesy to ask the girl's father for his consent. You should know his attitude toward you before you are engaged. Your approach to him will depend upon your familiarity with the family.

Your fiancée's parents will make the first announcement of the engagement, at a time and in a manner convenient to them. They will also give an announcement to the press, after which you may tell your friends. You will present your fiancée with an engagement ring, which is usually a diamond. The ring is a symbol of love and a declaration to marry the person to whom it is given. The one who wears the ring considers it a pledge to marry the giver. No other engagement gift can take the place of a ring.

An engagement is a serious obligation. Breach of promise is seldom enforced, but it is legal in many states. Do not become engaged unless you are in love and sincerely intend to marry.

The purpose of the engagement is to declare to all concerned that you have found the person whom you will marry. It is a period in which you prepare for your marriage by testing your love, making adjustments, plans and correcting faults.

After the engagement all old love affairs are merely memories. Both stop dating others. If the lovers are separated, any dates made to attend certain functions should be by mutual consent, with a third person known to you both or a person informed of your engagement. An engagement is meaningless unless dating ceases. A girl must become accustomed to the fact that her beloved will not always be able to go with her. A man who cannot be faithful to his betrothed seldom learns in marriage the meaning of fidelity. The engagement period is the time in which to prepare to live with one person for life.

There is a reality about the engagement. There is no need to attempt to impress the other or to be jealous. Instead of trying to exaggerate your worth, gracefully confess that you are not a "prize," after all. You will want to make certain that the one you are about to marry truly knows you. You will want to reveal your real self and be appreciated for what you are.

The engagement is a test of compatibility. You will both be privileged in asking for more of each other's time. You will seek every possible opportunity to know each other better and see how you react to various situations and demands. Complex situations, such as are peculiar to married life, should be faced together. A more intimate knowledge of each other than was possible in courtship days should now be gained. The fundamental question to be answered is: "Can we live happily together?"

Since personality is a prominent factor in one's happiness and his ability to make others happy, the engagement should be a time in which personality traits are discovered, discussed and determined. If there are undesirable traits, will the individual make an effort to correct them? Is he willing to read and study books on personality building? **Predicting Adjustment in Marriage from Adjustment in Engagement,** by E. W. Burgess and Paul Wallin[1], has proved amazingly accurate in its predications. **A Chart for Happiness,** by Hornell Hart, is a book founded on ten years of research and offers scientifically prepared charts whereby one may measure his happiness in relation to his life and work. It enables one to find his need for adjustment and suggests how to make corrections effectively. Prospective partners should read such studies together.

If you are happy as an engaged couple, it is reasonably certain that you will be happy with each other in marriage. The attitude, interests and comradeship found or strengthened in an engagement continue in marriage — as do the factors which irritate and offend.

The reactions of one partner toward the other will vary slightly, but married people see each other frequently, and the situation becomes permanent.

When there are faults and discrepancies in a personality, but a desire to correct them is evident, the same attitude will prevail in marriage. If no attempt is made to change the situation before marriage, that disposition will remain the same. The girl who marries a man to reform him or the man who dislikes certain traits in a girl but hopes she will change will invariably meet with disappointment. The time for correcting faults is the present.

Society recognizes the importance of an engagement and is free in commending the participants. Research shows

[1] **American Journal of Sociology,** Vol. 49, No. 4, January, 1944.

that the engaged couples are more likely to achieve happiness in marriage than those who went directly from courtship to marriage. Dr. Popenoe found that in a group of unhappily married persons 40 percent had not been engaged. They might have been acquainted for some time, but they were never officially engaged. Evidently they did not plan their marriages far in advance.

In the period of engagement, prospective mates should be candid in discussing their problems. The "give and take" spirit should be manifested clearly. Barriers that might possibly jeopardize happiness should be removed. If self-control is weak, the period of engagement is an ideal time to strengthen it. Emotional stability is a virtue to acquire. A desire to please and make progress must be exercised. Marriage is an important undertaking and the engagement period is the time to prepare for the best it can offer.

Common problems should be faced together, and gradually the prospective man and wife should acquire a complete understanding of what one will contribute and what is expected of the other. There should be a realization of a deepening sense of comradeship as plans and problems are discussed. Woodhouse[1] found that marital happiness depends upon "comradeship of husband and wife with congenial tasks and ideals, common interests and common friends, give and take, co-operation, confidence, understanding and frankness." The engagement period lends an opportunity to discover if your presence is indispensable to the other's happiness, if you can share ideas and ideals and work harmoniously toward a common goal.

When there are conflicting opinions and personality

1 Woodhouse, C. G., A Study of 250 Successful Families.

deficiencies which at first appear unsurmountable, talk freely about them. If you discover that you need assistance or counsel, visit your pastor. Many ministers are well equipped to give wise and sympathetic help. They will not betray your confidence, and will have your interest at heart. Do not fail to seek counsel before you become discouraged or disgusted. A little assistance from one who is familiar with the difficulties people face may save your engagement.

When you have discerned in your partner a weakness that you realize will mar your marriage, recall and recount his outstanding qualities. Consider the admirable traits, and against such a background place that which detracts from them. Discover your strength and weakness, kindness and selfishness and abilities and shortcomings, and offer mutual assistance in removing that which would impair the happiness of your marriage. Those who are happily married have learned to be of assistance to each other.

During the engagement, plans should be made regarding the date of the wedding, where to live and what equipment should be purchased in advance, but never should material interests crowd out love. Talk often of your love. If separated, write freely of your plans, but write most about your love. Any woman's heart will be stirred by a thoughtful love letter. Napoleon took time from cruel war to write beautiful letters to Josephine. Here are extracts from a letter which he wrote to her:

Marmirolo, July 17, 1796
9 o'clock P. M.
Dear Josephine:
    Since I left you I have been constantly depressed. My happiness is to be near you. Incessantly I live over in my memory your caresses, your tears, your affectionate solicitude. The charm of the incomparable Josephine kindles

continually a burning and a glowing flame in my heart. When free from all solicitude, all harassing care, shall I be able to pass all my time with you? . . . I thought I loved you months ago, but since my separation from you I feel that I love you a thousandfold more. Every day since I knew you have I adored you yet more and more. This proves the maxim of Bruyere, that "love comes all of a sudden," to be false. Everything in nature has its own course, and different degrees of growth.

Oh! I entreat you to permit me to see some of your faults. Be less beautiful, less gracious, less affectionate, less good; especially be not overanxious, and never weep. Your tears rob me of reason and inflame my blood. Believe me, it is not in my power to have a single thought which is not of thee, or a wish I could not reveal to thee.

Seek repose. Quickly re-establish your health. Come and join me, that at least, before death, we may be able to say, "We were many days happy!" A thousand kisses.

BONAPARTE

A love letter should disclose thoughts of affection and tenderness. Such a letter should not be "dashed off" in a hurry, but give evidence of time spent with the beloved through the medium of correspondence.

A letter to the person to whom you are engaged may tell what you have been doing and manifest an interest in the activities of your partner. Dwell on happy days that you have known together and express your desire that the time may soon come when you will be man and wife.

In-laws have an important relationship to every marriage. During the engagement period learn to know them intimately. Give yourself an opportunity to see and study their home life and family relationship. You can expect that your espoused will duplicate in a large measure the home environment out of which he has come.

How long should the couple be engaged? No specific time can be arbitrarily stated. The period should continue until the young people have had ample opportunity to test their comradeship and demonstrate their interests and desires. The time required will depend upon how long they have known each other and the duration of their courtship.

It is not commendable to become engaged when one has not the remotest idea when he can marry. It is better to extend the courtship period until there is some prospective date when marriage will be possible. Naturally, unforeseen obstacles may arise and must be considered, but it is wiser to prolong the courtship than to become engaged when plans for marrying are uncertain. The engagement period is not weakened by waiting, but it is jeopardized by stagnation. Lovers will wait as long as they are drawing nearer their goal. Time drags for the engaged only when there is no apparent evidence of progress toward the altar. Research is in favor of long engagements, as they give evidence of offering higher happiness in marriage. Long engagements are positively associated with a better adjustment in marriage than those which are brief. The longer the engagement the better the adjustment made in marriage, and the shorter the engagement the fewer are the possibilities for happiness.

Since research has revealed that those who have been engaged six months or less have a lower marital happiness score than couples engaged five years or longer it is conclusive that a sufficiently long engagement should be assured.

The matter of having a definite time in mind for marriage before becoming engaged need not conflict with a long engagement. One may set his goal for marriage and proceed toward it. Indefiniteness must be avoided. The number of months or years to wait is not a primary consideration. A couple may be engaged to marry as soon as he graduates from school. Others may hope to marry on a certain date, but loss of position or sickness may intervene. Should this be true, a new date must be set.

Those who are engaged for a year or more are usually moving toward a goal. People do not remain engaged for a long period of time unless they discover comradeship and a common purpose.

The duration of the courtship period, the problems to be solved, the time needed for the planning of a home and the common interests of the couple determine the length of time they should be engaged. Marriage should not take place until one is fully prepared for it.

There are two troublesome problems with which young engaged couples must deal. One is the question of disclosing personal and family secrets and the other concerns the degree of intimacy.

Any problem that persistently returns to your mind should be discussed. The fact that it demands your attention shows that your mind will not permit you to be at ease until you present it.

Take the problem that troubles you most and present it first. In this way you will eliminate many others. Once the question is presented, let it end there. Do not feel that you must "drag out another skeleton" unless the problem presents itself to your mind.

Facts that are fundamental should be stated, such as matters of health, legal entanglements or anything that could be told by a third party to dishonor you and undermine faith and confidence in you.

If you do not know how to present your perplexity,

consult your minister. He may be the one to plead your cause. Ask his advice, at any rate.

If there have been pre-marital sex relations it is wise to confess them. This is the price one must pay for indulgence. The man may or may not break the engagement. Even if he does, a girl will not be less happy without him than she would be with him. A woman will forgive a man for illicit relationships much quicker than a man will forgive a woman, even though a man is usually to blame. Yet I have known of successful marriages in which Christian men married women with a dark past, and they are happy. Before their marriages the women told their prospective husbands the history of their lives.

While in the service I often listened to young men talk about the type of girls they would marry. The question of illicit sex relations always became involved. The few men who voiced their willingness to marry girls who were "free with men" offered the reason that they were no better themselves. But men whose standards were low held the moral requirement high for the girls they desired to marry.

Statistics show that premarital sex relations undermine marital happiness. Correspondent with an increase in illicit sex practices is the increase in divorce resulting from maladjustment in marriage.

Engaged couples should remain pure. In the light of the evidence it is obvious that to indulge in undue intimacies impairs a couple's happiness and destroys the very purpose of the engagement: to lay the foundation for a happy and lasting marriage.

The advice of those who have given expression to their passion during the days of engagement is: "Don't do it!" Dr. Groves calls attention to a significant fact: "From information that has come to me through confidential consultation I am inclined to feel that it is the man, rather oftener than the woman, who in retrospect reacts to excessive freedom during the engagement, with antagonism or regret or even with a deep-seated suspicion of his life-partner, which makes affection difficult."

The fact that both of the engaged people may agree to sexual indulgence does not erase the feeling of guilt that follows. Nelson and Hiller[1] call attention to the fact that "sexual intercourse outside the socially accepted marriage conventions, even granted the integrity of the feeling each has for the other, involves serious hazards. The disapproval which society feels for this situation is heavy upon the violators of the code. Thus the feeling of guilt, the fear of being found out, the perpetual subterfuge necessary to secrecy, all contribute complicating factors to such a solution, coloring and making more difficult an adjustment that is at best sensitive and delicate. Moreover, under these conditions the sexual relationship instead of being part of a total experience and thus providing a strong and enduring foundation on which to build a rich and varied married life inevitably becomes something separate. Instead of finding increasingly intimate response at a variety of levels, and not the physical alone, the persons life becomes split up into many separate little pieces and parts, and no subsequent legalizing of the relationship in and of itself pulls them together again."

Some pseudo-intellectual persons attempt to justify promiscuousness during the engagement period on the ground that restraint would increase tension, nervousness and irritability and thus produce a neurotic state of mind. From

[1] Nelson, Janet F., and Hiller, Margaret, **Marriages Are Not Made in Heaven.**

a psychological point of view alone this assertion is based on a false premise. Fear of discovery and pregnancy will produce more anxiety than restraint will ever engender. Dr. Butterfield[1] writes that, "Cultural values being what they are in the present American setting, attempts at premarital sex experiences do more to produce sexual neurosis and personal maladjustment both before and after marriage than to relieve it." Nelson and Hiller contend that "establishment of the physical union may ease strain at the point of physical tension but may substitute strain at the point of the social and psychological adjustment." Since passion is aroused through the intimacy of the engaged couple, how can one deal most wisely with this natural desire?

1. **Anticipate, recognize and control the desire.** The desire in itself is not evil but natural. Man is to "replenish the earth." The passion is God-given. Do not try to hide your natural instincts, but make them subject to your will.

Self-control is a virtue that no one will find a burden. It is acquired through persistence and determination. The proper control of sexual desire is a healthy and wise way to develop moral restraint.

2. **Avoid sex-stimulating situations.** Thinking unduly about the importance of sex relations tends to arouse the desire.

Dr. Terman says that "our data do not confirm the view, so often heard, that the key to happiness is nearly always to be found in sexual compatibility. They indicate, instead, that the influence of sexual factors is at work no greater than that of the combined personality and background

1 Butterfield, Oliver, **The Love Problems of Adolescence.**

factors, and that it is probably less." Sex relationship is thus not a major problem to be considered.

Excessive caressing will arouse passion. Limits should, therefore, be set as safeguards and imposed by mutual consent. The couple should feel free to confide in each other about their sex urges and agree that whenever love-making causes unnecessary tension it must cease. Whatever caressing increases happiness and contentment is permissible, but that which threatens to jeopardize marital happiness should be prohibited.

During courtship the wise girl is stingy with her kisses. She saves them for the man she is to marry. The engagement implies the selection of that man. It is natural that the couple should express their affection for each other by caressing. Marriage permits an unrestricted intimacy in the expression of love.

3. **Self-control is aided by sublimation.** "When an emotion is displaced from a lower to a higher one, it is said to be sublimated."[1] Sublimation harnesses biological desires to spiritual and creative achievements. The couple can divert their sex urge into planning for their home or place these instinctive desires behind something that will enrich their companionship, interests and marital life. Music, art, athletics or building a house will provide a satisfying outlet for dynamic urges.

What if the engagement period of testing leads to dissatisfaction with the prospective partner? There is need for delayed action. Take time to see if the dissatisfaction is permanent. If a lack of certainty concerning love threatens to break the engagement, try dating others for a time or break off the engagement temporarily without

[1] Vaughn, Wayland, **General Psychology.**

publicizing the fact. One should make certain that he wants to break the engagement. If another person has entered the situation and has alienated the affection of one of the partners, the engagement has ceased in essence.

Both the engaged man and woman will find it advantageous to agree that should either find he has made the wrong choice they should separate without malice or hesitation.

When the engagement is to be broken, the girl makes the announcement to the public. She should not publicize details. Engagements are sometimes broken for no other reason than that one avoids setting a date for marriage. This engagement was not established in good faith; one either fears the responsibility of marriage or has found his companion unfitted for him. It is fair to break any engagement which offers little hope of marriage, or when one party refuses to fix a definite date for the wedding.

The broken declaration to marry should be looked upon as an experience that was entered into in good faith but was found to be unadvisable. There should be no brooding or marrying another "on the rebound." Those who follow a childish course of action injure no one but themselves.

A girl will suffer less criticism than the man if she breaks the promise. Other desirable girls may fear that he may not be trusted. Both partners should endeavor to make dates again with others, but should strive to be more cautious before becoming engaged again. If such a person is to profit from the experience gained, he should be able to make a wiser choice than the first time, especially if he desires to learn from experience.

PROBLEMS TO SOLVE BEFORE MARRIAGE

CHAPTER 8

Problems to Solve Before Marriage

There will be problems to face after marriage, as there will be joys to share, which one cannot anticipate and for which no specific preparation can be made, but if a young couple form the habit of facing difficulties together they will have developed one of the first prerequisites for a happy married life: companionableness.

Diverse problems will arise, but they will not be strangely new, since they will concern a couple who have learned to work together for each other's good. Adler[1] states that "the problems that we meet in love and marriage are of the same character as the general social problems. There

1 Adler, Alfred, **The Science of Living.**

are the same difficulties and the same tasks, and it is a mistake to regard love and marriage as a paradise in which all things happen according to one's desires. There are tasks throughout, and these tasks must be accomplished with the interests of the other person always in mind."

Problems that are bound to arise after marriage should be anticipated and studied sympathetically and patiently. What are some of these difficulties to face and settle during the engagement? A helpful answer can be found in studying the causes of dissatisfaction, unhappiness and maladjustment in marriage. Folsom[1] and Hamilton[2] present a helpful list which is too long to consider, but the more glaring causes should be studied. For convenience they may be considered as physical, social, emotional and m e n t a l problems.

1. The physical problems concern the health of the prospective bride and groom. Before marriage all questions relative to the health of both partners should be discussed frankly. If one has physical defects, will they become more pronounced with age, added strain and responsibility? Both should consult a competent physician and possess all the facts concerning the other's physical condition.

The question of health involves more than the care of a sick or invalid partner. It influences the financial situation, children in the home and in-law relationships.

A prospective bride may determine that she and her husband will meet the problem when they must face it, but the emotionally mature face problems in advance. For such people the words of Dr. Groves are pertinent. Speaking of the emotionally immature, he says, "Unwilling to look

1 Folsom, J. K., The Family.
2 Hamilton, G. V., A Research in Marriage.

squarely in the face the facts that concern them, and unequal to the demand put upon them to mature their choices, these men and women who refuse to travel emotionally out of childhood just cannot manage their lives successfully. Looking at their problems from a false background of distorted facts, and grasping satisfaction that cannot bring them abiding content, or even a considerable fulfillment of expectation, they misjudge and misuse every opportunity that comes to them for matrimonial and familial success."

Probably the most serious family difficulty arising from illness is the financial problem. The husband, in attempting to pay bills, will be forced to save money. The wife may charge him with meanness and the husband may accuse the wife of extravagance.

Should the woman need to supplement the family exchequer by working, there is always the possibility of inability to find a position. If the wife finds it imperative to work, the fear of pregnancy may result in a frigid wife or unnatural sexual relationships.

People marry "for richer or poorer or better or worse." When unforeseen illness or financial reverses arise, partners should be faithful to their vows, but it is wise to pay particular attention before marriage to the physical condition of a prospective partner. If your health or that of your partner is already failing, can you, and will you, begin your marriage knowing that ill health is soon to be your lot?

Many family quarrels are the direct result of financial conditions. Definite workable plans should be made before marriage as to the possibility and practicability of living as man and wife on one income. In the majority of cases, through careful planning and budgeting, the couple can reach a successful solution, but there should be an understanding about finances before the wedding. Two young people who have had most of their needs provided or who had their own earnings to spend should face realistically the restraint and self-denial that one income will impose upon them.

The question of attitude toward in-laws should be definitely settled. Do you like your in-laws? Statistics reveal that "difficulties caused by respective families" is a wrecking force with which to reckon.

Every possible attempt should be made to create and foster a congenial attitude toward in-laws and relatives. If your health fails, you may be obliged to live with them or they with you. Unless income warrants, no one should promise the other, "I will never ask my parents to live with us."

Young people will want to know how much salary they should receive and how much they should save before marriage. The answer will depend upon one's culture and social background. A farmer out of debt would be in a more favorable position than a man with a city home but no position. The girl who is accustomed to having money at her disposal may say, "Money never troubles me." She can say this when she has money, but what if she is denied it? Habitual practices are not easily altered, and what appears of little importance when one has always possessed it is paramount in the face of need.

Mowrer's[1] studies show that family finances rank first in the cause of divorce. Woodhouse[2] found that economic factors were the husband's first cause of worry and the

1 Mowrer, Ernest R., **Family Disorganization.**
2 Woodhouse, Chas. G., **A Study of 250 Successful Families.**

wife's second. Terman's research does not warrant the conclusion that a high income is essential if happiness is to be achieved in marriage, but the attitude that both husband and wife take toward their income is of primary importance. The important point is that during the engagement the fact must be faced and an attempt be made to agree, before marriage, on making the most of the income available.

As a result of counseling and questionnaires Dr. Groves offers the following advice gleaned from the experience of young married couples who have "gone through" the first stages of marriage. This is a partial list.

Do not buy on the time-payment plan.

Do not marry on less than $2,500 a year.

Marry without debt and with some reserve.

Have a complete understanding of the husband's income and obligations.

Save at least 10 percent regardless of income.

Have a budget that suits and stick to it.

Don't do unnecessary installment buying.

Save regularly from the beginning.

Face the income and standard of living before marriage.

If possible, live alone and not with relatives.

Pay as little as possible for an apartment the first year or two.

The above recommendations may serve as a guide for young people about to marry.

If a wife must take a position, her doing so should be considered an emergency effort and not a permanent plan. One fact should never be forgotten: children born into the home need a mother's care. A nurse cannot do for a child what a mother can do to make his life beautiful, and a competent maid cannot equal what a wife can do for the happiness and comfort of her home and husband. A woman's reward for putting her time and interest into her home is her husband's praise and unfaltering love.

The attitude of both the man and the woman toward sex should be discussed freely. Maladjusted sex life causes considerable marital conflict. Sex life is more than physical union: it is a spiritual relationship. This is a truth that many books on sex fail to recognize. Many of these well-meaning authors give an important place to the mechanics of sex life but ignore the importance of the proper attitude toward it.

The Bible exercises a wholesome frankness in dealing with this question of sex relations — a frankness which should make us ashamed of our prudishness. Our silence is perhaps a result of the unwholesome manner in which we have received sex education or heard the subject discussed.

The Christian Church has not followed the example of the Bible in its discussion of sex. The Church is the only place where the subject is not discussed. Theaters, clubs, places of amusement, schools and street corners are centers from which circulates misleading and inelegant sex information. Vulgar terms are often used to describe any relationship involving sex. Even some pastors ignore certain passages of Scripture because they deal with the subject. Recently as I sat in church I heard the story of the new birth read from Scripture. When the reader came to John 3:4 he omitted the verse. He then encouraged his listeners to read the lesson at home. Will they wonder why he avoided this one verse?

The church is the one place where sane and discriminating sex instruction can be given. Young married couples, or engaged people, should have a Christian understanding and appreciation of the place which sex has in their lives.

Many ministers are prepared to offer helpful courses in sex education — courses that would save many boys and girls from an undesirable response to this biological urge. Marriage would be saved from discord if both parties knew the Christian teaching regarding sex, but would their churches tolerate such studies?

The Christian Church must realize its duty and, instead of evading the subject, let youth know what the Bible has to say about this important phase of life. Let the Church not make the mistake of considering this another "project," but, rather, let it view the issue as one of the subjects that must be faced. The words of Archibald Henderson apply to the need for Christian sex instruction. He says, "Untutored thinking is less than useless today. It is dangerous and harmful in a world bristling with ideas worked out by scholars and experts." Readers of this book can do much, for the sake of those who are younger, to encourage wholesome sex education in their churches.

An admirable book[1] written jointly by a man and a woman offers a sane appraisal of the marital relationship: "The complete sex relationship will involve, in the case of cultured people, not only the whole personality but the whole of both personalities. Psychologically, the sex act involves the mutual 'transference', absorption, of the two concerned —a completeness of self-giving and other accepting. This is possible only where intimate acquaintance and great respect, permanence and affection are present. The sex act receives its specifically human meaning from the accompanying elements in it which are not directly sexual; then obviously the richness of the sex experience will depend to a large extent on the number and quality of experiences, both sexual and non-sexual, that the couple have had together. This explains the increasing beauty and

[1] Elliott, Grace L., and Bone, Harry, The Sex Life of Youth.

satisfaction of the experience to those who have been lovers for many years. This is why real marriage most adequately fulfills the conditions for the true satisfaction of human sex hunger."

It is imperative that engaged couples be thoroughly familiar with each other's attitude toward sex. They should approach the issue as they would approach any other problem which if not wisely handled could mar their marriage.

Sex is one of the basic urges of life and finds its expression in affection and love. It cannot be completely divorced from the physical desire, as Hindu philosophers once contended, nor does it dominate the whole of life, as Freud taught. It is both physical and spiritual. It should be discussed until a rational conclusion is reached, like any other important matter involved in marriage. Sane and helpful books in this field are suggested in the last chapter of this volume. Every engaged couple should read one or more of them. It is necessary that they read sufficiently to develop a normal and agreeable attitude toward the importance of the relationship in their marriage. It is wise first for them to read together a book that covers the entire field of marital obligations; then they should read specific volumes as needed. These general books are also listed in this volume.

Social or cultural difficulties should be anticipated. It is evident that there will be cultural differences to solve. There are customs and family traditions over which one has little conscious control. There are fixed habits which grow out of social background. Attitudes toward the home and the marital partner have been fairly fixed and colored by the home training of each individual.

Social differences will have a large influence in deciding where one should live. It may be difficult for a farm boy to become enthusiastic over a city girl's desire to live in an apartment house in the center of a bustling city.

At the beginning young people should recognize the different backgrounds that influence their behavior, likes and feelings, and they should face the facts candidly and consistently.

Dr. Swindler[1] has named cultural differences between the marriage partners as a second cause that leads to marital breakdown. He states that "background, habits and traditions seem of little significance when young people are attracted to each other . . . Later these differences show themselves in their real importance. Even if two young people were able to emancipate themselves completely from their respective families and the group in which they have grown up, they cannot escape themselves. From earliest childhood every individual has been patterned in countless little details by the culture of his group. His speech, the way he likes his food, his esthetic standards, his mores, his observance of the holidays and national customs were established long before he was conscious of the process by which he was conditioned . . . The individual has little conscious control over these features of his personality."

Rating high as causes of divorce are "nerves," lack of co-operation and independence. In families where partners were dissatisfied with mates the score which registered lack of harmony was high because of disagreements, lack of sympathy and the presence of personality defects. Many of these difficulties could be attributed to the difference in cultural backgrounds. It is important, then, that young engaged couples study each other's background and discuss, for their future happiness, the seriousness of the differences

1 Schindler, Carl J., *The Pastor as a Personal Counselor.*

that are displeasing and which will undoubtedly later become a source of annoyance, resulting in "nerves". If no agreement can be reached or if there is unwillingness to work toward correcting the undesirable traits, there will be dissatisfaction in marriage. By recognizing these defects, both the person who possesses them and the partner in marriage are preparing for the happiness that should be theirs. When no attempt is made to correct faults, the person who dislikes them knows that they exist and may seek other qualities in the partner which are so highly commendable that he is still first choice. Desirable traits can then be accentuated, and others, still a source of annoyance, can be minimized. The dissatisfaction is thus lessened but is aggravated at times.

Such acts as fits of temper, uncontrolled conduct, moodiness, crying and undue display of physical strength in closing doors and handling dishes are evidences of emotional immaturity.

One who has emotional maturity has the ability to make decisions, to "give and take," lose and win without depression or elation. He will discuss problems coolly and calmly and weigh their value. He will not seek to dominate, will take his share of responsibility willingly, will not be disagreeable when disappointed and develop a constructive rather than a critical state of mind.

The engaged couple can help each other to grow emotionally. You mature emotionally as you turn to your problems and out of them evolve a solution that applies to your particular needs. This is one reason why you can read books on marriage and yet fail in it. Success in marriage is achieved not by the adoption of plans from an outside source but by accepting guidance and by its direction facing your own problem and finding an answer that is peculiarly your own. Emotional maturity is realized through discovery for one's self that a certain policy is wise and practical. That knowledge then becomes a part of one's personality.

You may go to a lecture and hear that your digestion is harmed when you quarrel with your sweetheart while you are dining, but nevertheless you quarrel with him the next time you eat. If you decide or agree that it is childish to quarrel over the trivial matters that arouse you and that you are an adult and will treat quarrels as infantile, you have grown emotionally. Emotional growth is also evident when reasoning replaces shouting, entreaties and tears, and when emotional outbursts are recognized as childish.

If a young couple will, facing the real issues that can stand in the way of their marital happiness, look at each other's faults without attempting to justify or excuse them, but resolve by mutual assistance to correct them, they need have no fear that an emotional disturbance will mar their marital bliss. If you cannot plan to live together pleasantly and lovingly in marriage, you will be happier if you remain single and wait until you "grow up". Most of the complaints that husbands and wives make concerning each other are the result of emotional immaturity. Some of the major grievances which husbands hold against their wives are found by Terman and others to be "nagging, criticizing, feelings too easily hurt, quick-tempered and conceited." The wives charge the husbands with "selfishness, nervousness, impatience, complaining, uncommunicativeness and touchiness." All these characteristics are evidences of lack of emotional stability.

Tension or mental strain is a prominent cause of quarrels

and unhappiness in marital relationships. It may demonstrate itself in fear, anxiety or worry. Women complain of their husbands' failure to consider them or take them into their confidences. Unrest may rise from a lack of freedom or inability to cope with a situation or a "shut in" feeling. Space is not provided to exercise one's freedom or that freedom is denied. The cause of this feeling is mental. A basic need is not being satisfied. The accusation that one is not consulted by the partner shows a feeling of lack of significance. The partners can relieve this situation by being companionable, sharing interests, proceeding on a "fifty-fifty" basis, respecting personal opinions, "giving in" when nonessentials are involved, and doing things together. Lack of co-operation is sometimes called mental cruelty. A couple can remedy this situation by deciding together how they want things done.

I recall a man who asked a woman's opinion about a certain matter. She voiced her view willingly. It was not the answer he wanted, and so he attempted to persuade her. She held her ground admirably. Eventually he said, "Well, let's do it my way this time." When he left she said, "He seldom takes my advice when he wants to do something, but he always asks me what I think." Wise woman! She gave her consent and was thankful that her husband always sought it even though he acted to please himself.

Much of the mental strain which married couples experience is a result of the fact that one of the partners does not know what the other is going to do or what he thinks about matters that are important to both. The lack of freedom, of which both husband and wife complain, and disagreement about amusements reflect a lack of interest in each other. These grievances arise when two people live together but resemble boarders in a house rather than joint proprietors.

It is interesting to observe that the Gallup Poll[1] revealed that men and women have changed little in their marital faults. From coast to coast the poll-takers questioned 3,100 men and women "from newlyweds to great-grand-mothers," and men of all ages and stations in life. The ten chief faults of their husbands, according to the wives, are, in order of importance: "Drinking, thoughtlessness or lack of consideration, selfishness — thinking only of themselves; too domineering — bossy; other women, stinginess, lack of interest in the house, take you for granted, complaining too much, gambling and smoking." What have the men to say about their wives? They charge them with, in order of their severity, "nagging, (driving you to drink) extravagance, poor homemaker, too much night club and drinking, gossiping, selfishness, too many outside interests, too bossy, careless and untidy personally, and other men."

The chief grievance against husbands was drinking. Drinking is usually a defense mechanism or a form of neurosis or psychosis. Men drink to escape reality rather than face it. Although a few of the grievances of both men and women are based on physical limitations or offenses, most of them are due to emotional immaturity. They have similar faults but their interests are not common. If the husbands drink the wives evidently do not, or the drinking wives do not have drinking husbands. At any rate, their drinking is not a common bond of interest. Common interests never unite a man and wife if such interests are on a low moral plane and are fraught with after effects that arouse suspicion and destroy respect.

1 Lydgate, Wm. A., Red Book, June, 1946.

An engaged couple would find it helpful to check their faults against this list and eliminate all undesirable elements.

It is wise for a married couple to remember the pleasure they had as lovers planning their marriage. Every happy association which they, as man and wife, can recall which occurred during their engagement, strengthens their love and happiness.

WILL THERE BE CHILDREN ?

CHAPTER 9

Will There Be Children?

Only a few years ago an unmarried couple would be considered immodest, if not immoral, if they spoke of their sex relationship when married. Even after marriage such matters were not discussed by "nice" people, though wives gave birth to children.

The reason for such undue modesty was this: sex was considered too sacred or too evil to be discussed by "decent" people. There are times today when this unwholesome modesty would be preferable to the loose, nonintellectual chatter, bordering on the obscene, which is heard in some circles. Neither practice, however, is commendable.

Progressive thinking regarding marital problems develops

155

slowly. This was true also of other attempts to improve living conditions. Bathtubs were once frowned upon, for example. Queen Elizabeth scandalized England by having her own tub installed and by bathing in it once a month, whether she needed a bath or not.

People were slow to accept the advancements made in medical science. Cotton Mather's life was threatened because he instructed a physician that it would be morally right to vaccinate his son against smallpox. Anesthesia, as well as vaccination, was condemned.

Customs do not change easily, and it is fortunate that society does not gullibly accept every innovation. Yet refusal to evaluate evidence and weigh facts leads to stagnation.

Young people planning marriage should talk reverently and sincerely about that which is related to their marital happiness. One important question is: Will there be children? The time to decide this issue is before marriage, during the engagement period. Dr. Groves declares that "only the immature and irresponsible person will shy away from bringing out into the open a question that may become, when it is covered up, a cause of reproach and dissatisfaction in later married life."

By declaring before marriage his position for or against children in the home one can settle a problem that may wreck a marriage which otherwise would be happy. Dr. Popenoe found in "a recent study in an Eastern state that of the couples who were permanently childless, a majority claimed to be unhappy over the fact; often indeed it was the greatest tragedy of their lives." Two people who plan to have their own home should know what children mean to them. There is nothing but disappointment in store for a

woman who marries a man who differs fundamentally from
her regarding children. A fact to be reckoned with is that
one out of every five American wives has never borne a
child. If the wife cannot have children, how would the
husband react? This has always proved to be a problem.
The ancients solved the difficulty by marrying another wife.
Men in Biblical times were permitted to rear families
through concubines or servants, as Abraham did, but this
usually resulted in unhappiness.

It is estimated that approximately 22.6 percent of the
wives who do not give birth to children are sterile and that
70.4 percent are relatively sterile, but no wide study has
been made to establish an accurate percentage. It might,
however, become necessary for a couple to remain childless
or adopt a child. Would both agree to adoption?

The question of children should be freely discussed by
the engaged couple. Harris warns that "nowhere will the
possession of divergent views cause more troubles than in
the realm of sex and the bringing up of children. A great
deal can be found out about the attitude of 'both' in these
matters before engagement, but there is a sense in which
the engagement itself forms the best opportunity for
mutual understanding . . . if after everything that can be
done has been done, a man and a woman find themselves
basically disagreed on the physical expression of love or on
the way to bring up children, the chances are that they
should not marry each other."[1] The problem of sex and
children in the home should be discussed and considered
like any other subject that relates itself to marital happiness.

A couple will not advance far in the question, "Will there

1 Harris Erdman, Twenty-One

be children?", until they discuss the number of children desired. This introduces the problem of birth control.

The following discussion of birth control, or regulated families, is not to advance any theory but to urge young people about to marry to give serious attention to what childbearing involves. Supported by knowledge and their convictions, they should agree on a plan that will not harm their bodies, minds or souls. The counsel of Ralph Blount[1] is that a couple enter marriage with a plan even if they later find a better one which they will adopt.

We approach the problem of regulating the family's size in the spirit of Dr. Nash[2] who wrote, "Happily there is a growing conviction that there is no longer (indeed, never was) any obligation to make a 'correct' (i. e., rigorist) attitude toward birth control a test of orthodoxy . . . All that may rightly be demanded by Christian people is that they should be ready to think honestly and courageously, with all the evidence before them, and that they allow clear moral principles, and not prejudices or fear, to determine their judgment. "

Some knowledge of the background of the modern birth-control movement may prove enlightening. It had its beginning in England in 1798 when an economist, Thomas Robert Malthus, wrote an essay entitled "Essay of the Principle of Population as It Affects the Future Improvement of Society." In this treatise he raised the question of poverty due to increased population. In 1803 he brought out a bolder declaration of his thesis and argued that overpopulation could be remedied by moral restraint and late marriage. Late marriage would reduce the population by the limited number of offspring that could result from

1 Blount, R., Love Loyal.
2 Nash, A. S., Education for Christian Marriage.

the union. This was a definite recommendation to reduce
the size of the family. Such a procedure is birth control.

In 1822 the labor leader Francis Place was accused of
publishing an anonymous leaflet which was branded "The
Diabolical Handbill." It contended for regulated families to
aid the poor. Place was held in contempt for this thesis.

Richard Carlile (1790-1843), an English free thinker,
defied the regulated press and spent three years in jail
because he wrote the first English book contending for the
use of contraceptives by married people. In 1833, an
American, Dr. Charles Knowlton, wrote the first American volume on the subject, but gave it the title **Fruits
of Philosophy.** His book was read secretly. Mrs. Gernit
Van Deth, better known as Margaret E. Sanger, while a
New York nurse, became intensely interested in the birth-
control movement for the good of humanity. The American
Birth Control League was established in 1915 largely
through her efforts.

The birth-control movement has never advocated childless marriages when health and security would permit
children. It has advocated proper spacing of children and
limiting the number of offspring when to do so was in the
best interest of parent and child. It has not advised coer-
cion but the making available of scientific methods, upon
the advice of their physicians, for mothers who need
assistance.

The advocates of birth control have zealously entreated
that children should be planned for and that they should
bless every young married couple's union.

Quacks and unscrupulous promoters have made it appear
"smart" not to have children. They have made the birth-
control question offensive, and their profiteering attitude

has done much to make a discussion of the subject distasteful. Advertisements have indirectly or directly placed a cloud of immodesty over the subject. If you were more than twenty-one, you could purchase, through the mail with no name on the label but your own, a book that would disclose the dark secrets of "what you should know."

The above type of advertising and literature is not to be confused with the birth-control movement sponsored by Margaret Sanger and others. One must remember also that birth control is not abortion. It desires to abolish abortions, to prevent conception and, therefore, pregnancy by scientific contraceptive measures. It does not desire to abolish the family but to determine the time of the birth of a child and regulate proper spacing between children.

The sane advocates of birth control are in thorough agreement that marriage carries with it the responsibilities of a family. They advise against childless marriages and warn that the sex life of a man and his wife does not consist merely of pleasure. One doctor[1] contended that marital sex relations are more than pleasure functions but are spiritual communion of man and wife. Dr. Marie Stopes[2] wrote that "my object is not to make sex expression a dangerous free indulgence, but to raise the sense of responsibility, the standard of self-control and knowledge which goes with maturity, and consequently the ultimate health and happiness of those who mate . . . a family of healthy, happy children should be the joy of every pair of married lovers." Dr. Long[3] and Dr. Robinson[4] contend that children are necessary for a complete home and the highest attainment

1 Stone, Chester T., *Sexual Power.*
2 Wise Parenthood.
3 Long, H. W. (M.D.), *Sane Sex Life and Sane Sex Living.*
4 Robinson, William (M.D.), *Women.*

of human living and advises against not planning for children. The Groves[1] have always argued in favor of rearing a family born by choice.

The aforementioned works are by trustworthy authors and may be read safely by engaged couples without fear of unchaste language or prejudiced arguments. They are written to give information, not to advance methods.

The birth-control advocates took cognizance of the fact that the question is no longer "Will birth control be practiced?" but "what is the safest and sanest method to use?" They saw abuses, loss of life and marital unhappiness caused through ignorance of proper methods, and they observed the tragedy of the unwanted child in a home overpopulated with children. They proposed to correct such conditions by trustworthy and scientific devices used upon recommendation of family physicians.

Before World War II, 375,000,000 prophylactics were sold annually in the United States. Sale of contraceptive methods not approved by the Birth Control Federation had reached a total of $250,000,000 annually. Abortions, which are not to be confused with contraceptives, were being performed at the rate of 700,000 a year, resulting in 8,000 known deaths. The majority of abortions were not performed on unwed mothers, but approximately 90 percent were performed on married women, especially wives between the ages of twenty-five and thirty-five, who already had a number of children.

The claim of the birth-control promoters, namely, that they were advocating a sane and scientific method in order to abolish unscientific and health-jeopardizing schemes that were widely used, is founded upon fact. The research

1 Groves, Ernest R., and Gladys H., *Sex and Marriage.*

conducted by Hamilton, Davis, Dickenson and Pearl supports their conviction.

Research shows that as many as 90 percent of married women employ contraceptives, and only half the number are fully satisfied with the methods they use. Twenty-one percent of the latter report having had one or more abortion.

A consensus[1] taken among 4,500,000 married couples in America shows that four-fifths of them use some method of birth control and 77 percent favor government birth-control clinics.

The changing economic life in America has increased the problems of a couple who desire to have all the children the mother is able to bear. In past years children were a financial asset to a farmer's family, but with the coming of tractors and other powerful machinery manpower was greatly reduced.

It is estimated that the average cost, based on prewar figures, to rear a child from birth to the age of eighteen is $5,036. The amount is more than treble for parents with an income of more than $5,000 annually.

The health of the mother and children already born is another factor to be considered. There are times when the birth of another child may prove detrimental to the mother's health, or cause the children to be undernourished because the income is not sufficient to feed more members of the household. Protestants, in general, are convinced that a wife has a right to live and that her life should not be forfeited for the purpose of giving birth to a child she cannot live to rear. The Catholic position is clearly defined by Pope Pius XI in an encyclical which states, "Any use whatsoever

1 **Ladies' Home Journal** Survey, 1938.

of matrimony exercised in such a way that the act is deliberately frustrated in its natural power to generate life is an offense against the law of God and of nature, and the guilt of a grave sin." The encyclical states further that this regulation is enforced and not to be ignored even if pregnancy proves fatal to the mother.

The Catholic position on birth control is decidedly one of opposition. The method is considered unnatural and intrinsically evil.

It may be wise to enumerate the arguments advanced against and in favor of birth control. By birth control is meant the use of mechanical measures to prevent conception. Those against it contend —

1. That it is unnatural, in that it distorts the sex act from its original purpose: pregnancy.

2. That it is anticipated murder, in that it makes impregnation or conception impossible, thus preventing the birth of a child.

3. That it degrades the marital status by encouraging legalized prostitution between husband and wife and destroys self-control.

4. That a knowledge of safe birth-control methods would corrupt youth by removing the fear of pregnancy.

The answers to these charges are:

1. Birth control is unnatural, but so are pasteurization, vaccination, hygiene and many modern conveniences. To reject birth control as unnatural is to be either inconsistent or prejudiced.

2. If it is murder to guard against the conception of children through birth control, then continency, the rhythmic method and failure to rear all the children one can have are also forms of murder.

3. It does not degrade but elevates the marital relationship by showing regard for the welfare of the mother and the family. It gives a man and wife an opportunity to express this affection and love without fear.

4. If so minded, youth will use contraceptive means. The "absence of knowledge is never so erroneous as the abuse of ignorance." Those who refrain from sexual indulgence through fear only have already lusted in their hearts. Training in birth control will eliminate a great deal of superstition and ignorance concerning the place of sex relationship in marriage. The knowledge of safe and scientific methods would turn youth to early marriage and lessen premarital sex relationships.

The Catholic Church disapproves unequivocally of birth control but does not disapprove of family limitation by the rhythmic method. Pope Pius XI, in an encyclical dated December 31, 1931, on Christian marriage, approved the rhythmic method in restricting the size of the family. He reasoned: "They are not acting against the order of nature, if they make use of their rights according to sound and natural reasons, even though no new life can thence arise on account of circumstances or time or the existence of some defect." This ruling admits that marital sex relationship is permissible without anticipated parenthood.

The "safe period" or rhythmic period has been advocated as early as the second century. In brief, it states that there are certain periods in a month in which impregnation is impossible. There is considerable difference in opinion as to when this period is. One of the best discussions on the subject is obtainable in leaflet[1] form for twenty-five cents.

1 Robinson, Wm. J., **The Safe Period.** Published by Eugenics Publishing Co., New York City.

With the Catholic Church's approval of the "safe period" a new type of profiteering came into vogue. Quacks offered to determine, for a small fee, the "safe period" for every woman who would subscribe to their course of analysis and diagnosis. Sane and reliable workers have been overshadowed by the misleading advertisers, but science is still searching for a reliable answer.

The difference between regulating the size of one's family by unscientific (rhythmic) and scientific (birth control) measures is difficult to determine. Both advocates appear to agree that a man and wife are not required to rear as many children as could possibly be conceived.

The purpose of birth control, then, is not to advocate childless marriages but to plan for a wanted rather than an unanticipated child or children. Dr. T. W. Galloway[1] contends that "in general it seems humane and reasonable that no family should have more children than it can bring into the world without disastrous effects upon the life and health and cultural opportunities of the mother, that it can nourish and keep in health during dependence, that it can provide with an education and a basis for self-support and success . . . This means voluntary parenthood, not as a protection of selfishness and license, but as an aid to intelligent, scientific and humane promotion of home conditions, personal perfection, social welfare and racial progress."

The teachings of all churches have been in support of a family and against childless marriages. Many Protestant denominations do not disfavor the limiting of the size of the family when physical conditions warrant such action. This view is well expressed by Dr. Edwin Dahlberg[2] in a

1 Love and Marriage.
2 Youth and the Home of Tomorrow.

book that is still one of the best on Christian marriage. He writes, "I would not stand in opposition to restriction of the size of the family when the health of the mother or the miseries of the home demand it. Economic want, social despair, physical disability, even the pursuance of a college education, may all be legitimate reasons for the postponement or limitations of parenthood. But some of our young married people should seriously resist the present overemphasis on unnecessary childlessness."

The action of the Anglican Church in Great Britain is fairly representative of the Protestant attitude in America toward the place of children in the home. The Church contended that it was immoral to avoid having children for selfish motives, but it was surely, also, immoral to have child after child under circumstances which, humanly speaking, were such as to render the proper upbringing of such children impossible. The Church had earlier approved of limiting childbearing when the health of the mother was endangered by another baby.

To guard against unnecessary delay in rearing a family a wife should remember that the ages between twenty and twenty-nine are her most favorable years for childbearing and, also, that there is one situation worse than too many children and that is no child or children. The admonition of Bell Wiley[1] should be taken seriously: "Set your time for your first child in the beginning and let nothing short of financial catastrophe postpone it."

The coming of a child offers an opportunity for both parents to increase their devotion and love to each other and center that love around one of their own flesh and blood.

1 So You Are Going to Get Married.
2 What Life Should Mean to You.

Adler[2] wrote that "love, with its fulfillment, — marriage, — is the most intimate devotion toward a partner of the other sex, expressed in physical attraction, in comradeship and in the decision to have children." Your love never finds its true fulfillment until a child is born to you.

John W. Coutts, in his provocative book, **The Church and the Sex Question** places upon the husband and wife the problem of rearing a family. He reasons thus: "It looks to be a thorough Christian proposition that husband and wife should agree as to the most solemn act they ever jointly undertake, the act by which a new life is started upon the career which contains within it the potency of becoming eternally a child of God."

Remember that marriage is a divine institution. If you desire to find the highest and best in it, seek the help and counsel of your church, and in the words of Shakespeare, may "God, the best maker of all marriages, combine your hearts in one, your home in one."

PLANNING YOUR WEDDING

CHAPTER 10

Planning Your Wedding

A woman's wedding is the crowning hour of her life. From childhood she talks of the time when she will be married. Men and women look forward to marriage and having a home of their own, but women talk more about this dream. Men approach the matter more realistically than women, who associate it closely with romance. It is still considered an achievement for a woman to have "gotten her man."

Courtship is a carefree period, but not void of fear — fear of not finding the right person, and after finding him, the possibility of losing him. When the engagement period follows, planning begins, and with the approaching wedding day comes added excitement and anticipation. The engage-

ment is important, but the wedding is paramount. It is
the one event in life that must be meaningful.

On her wedding day a woman changes her name. She
assumes a new status, as does her husband, in society. She
is no longer "Miss" but "Mrs." If her husband is famous
or well known in the community, his prestige and attainment becomes hers through marriage.

Men are not so thrilled by the anticipation of the wedding
day as are women. It is difficult for a man to view the
wedding as enchanting, bewitching and thrilling. He will
probably be more excited than the bride, but he will not be
as thrilled as she.

The problems involved in the marital status and the practical difficulties that must be confronted in providing for a
household are probably foremost in the man's mind. He
may love as deeply or deeper than the bride, but he is not
as romantic as she. It is wise for the woman to bear these
facts in mind and not charge her espoused with showing
indifference or lack of love if he is not "thrilled to death."
There will be no need to ask him if he does not realize that
"we are being married tomorrow."

When the engagement is announced, plans for the date
of marriage should be made. This decision may be contingent
upon certain factors that make the date somewhat indefinite.
The wedding date may depend upon completing an education or finding a place to live. If this be so, the public announcement of the engagement should read, "No definite
date has been set for the wedding." Make no attempt to
explain why. That is the concern of those involved.

The length of the engagement, as stated earlier, will be
determined by the length of the courtship, the frequency
of association and the problems to be solved before marriage.

An engagement should be longer than a few months in duration to allow for proper essential adjustments, that are prerequisite to a long and happy marriage

When the prospective husband is ready to marry and has made all the arrangements necessary for setting up a new home, he will inform his bride. If the two have worked closely together, she will be aware of the progress made. He will not determine the date of the wedding but state that after a certain time he will be ready. The bride then sets the wedding date, which should be selected from one to six months in advance of the marriage. If she cannot be ready within this time she should not select a specific day but simply decide to marry in a certain month.

After the bride has set the date for her wedding, and the groom has agreed, they should decide on where they will be married and by whom. The groom must bear in mind that it will be the bride's wedding. He may say, "It is my wedding, too," but the bride and her parents have the chief responsibility of the occasion, and it is the young lady's privilege to plan it as she pleases.

Religious differences may prohibit the bride from being married where she desires. A Catholic cannot marry a non-Catholic and have a church wedding, and divorcees are not permitted to marry in some churches. The place where the marriage is to take place should be decided by the bride and approved by the groom. Agreement on this point is essential. Should there be a sharp difference it is feasible to postpone the date of marriage until all concerned agree on the place selected.

Before she makes plans, a Catholic girl should inform a Protestant that she cannot have a church wedding unless the man becomes Catholic. Men have been known to turn

Catholic upon short notice of the church's stand, and later have not conducted themselves as devout Catholics. A similar problem arises when a non-Christian refuses to be married in a Christian church. Some men may want the marriage performed, not solemnized, by a friend who is a justice of the peace.

The question as to who will perform the sacrament of marriage, and where, should not be left unanswered until the last minute of the engagement period. Wise plans, made far in advance of the marriage, will prevent unnecessary anxiety, quarreling and disappointment. If the bride's plans are reasonable, they should be complied with cheerfully. If she has a church home, her minister is the logical person to perform the ceremony. Wise clergymen will refuse to come into any church to perform a marriage for even "an old friend of the family" where a resident minister is located. The pastor of the church where the bride is a member should perform the service. The groom should not ask his minister to assist when the partners belong to different churches.

Only one person performs the marriage. The individual who receives the vows, pronounces the couple man and wife and is held responsible for filing the return of the marriage with the authorities issuing the license.

When the date for the wedding has been tentatively agreed upon by the partners, the prospective bride, alone or with her mother, engages the minister and the church. Having received assurance that the clergyman and the church are available, the young lady, with her mother or guardian, makes plans for the wedding. They decide on the announcements and invitations and to whom they will be sent. The groom is consulted regarding the number of friends of his family whom he should like invited to his wedding.

The expenses of preparation for the wedding is borne by the bride's parents. They should decide, with her, whether the wedding is to be formal or informal, and should agree upon the amount of money to be spent on the preparations and reception. They also provide the bride with her trousseau and it is their responsibility to provide floral decorations at the church and home and bouquets for the bride's attendants, pay the fees for the church organist, the soloist and the sexton, make arrangements for photographs of the bridal party, supply the wedding cake, and purchase a gift from the members of the bride's family.

The groom pays for the marriage license, the wedding ring, a wedding gift for his bride, and gifts to his best man and ushers, in addition to their wedding ties and boutonnieres and the clergyman's honorarium.

Clergymen do not charge for performing marriages, and whatever they receive is a gift from the groom. The money should be placed in an envelope and given to the minister by the best man before or after the wedding. The minister presents to the bride a marriage certificate that may have cost him from one to five dollars. He will also mail to the proper authorities a report of the marriage. The gift varies from five to twenty dollars, depending upon the locality and generosity of the groom.

State and county laws regulate the granting of marriage licenses. Whether the law requires it or not, it is wise for both partners to apply for the license together. There are questions about names that only the person concerned may be able to furnish. Clergymen can usually give the information necessary for licenses and may be consulted if one is not familiar with the legal marital requirements.

If the bride is planning a church wedding, she, or her mother, may make the plans for the ceremony. The size of the bridal party will depend on where the ceremony takes place. If it is performed in the church, there will be more attendants than those required for a parish house or parsonage wedding.

Even though the marriage be a quiet ceremony in the home or parsonage, it is wise for the bride and groom to have two attendants. A bridegroom has his best man, who is usually a brother, close relative, best friend or bride's brother. A sister of the bride, near her age, is usually the maid of honor. If she does not have a sister, she selects a relative or friend.

Where one is married in a parsonage the service is referred to as "a marriage," not "a wedding." Friends should be at the manse not later than fifteen minutes before the marriage. The bride and groom should arrive at the stated hour. They should not go to their wedding together but they may go to their marriage in each other's company.

Wedding announcements are not invitations to a wedding, but an acknowledgment of acquaintanceship. One should not attend a wedding on the strength of an announcement. Announcements and invitations should be mailed approximately three weeks in advance of the wedding.

Wedding gifts should be recorded in an appropriate book, then exhibited carefully and thoughtfully in a room where they can be seen to advantage. Checks or money should not be on display. All gifts should be acknowledged in the bride's own handwriting as soon as possible after the wedding.

When one is planning a church wedding there will be the necessity of one or more rehearsals, for which the clergy-man will arrange. As the entire function is the responsibility of the bride and her parents, the minister will not volunteer suggestions but will render invaluable service if requested. He can spare the bride many details and much worry if she, or her mother, solicits his assistance.

A bride may desire to inform herself regarding the proper etiquette for weddings. Among the most helpful books on this subject is **Etiquette,** by Emily Post.

A wedding should be as meaningful and beautiful as possible. It should be a fond memory to which both bride and groom return happily after many years of married life. Blessing upon blessing will enrich their marriage if the couple can recall their wedding as one of happiest days of their lives, unmarred by mistakes and misunderstandings through wise planning.

Secret weddings are not acceptable. Society frowns upon them and the feelings of parents and in-laws are usually injured. Many of those who married secretly have regretted their action. More than once I have heard the sad story of a young couple who were displeased with their secret marriage or elopement and wanted to know how they could be married in a dignified and reverent manner. One said, "The whole affair was revolting and offensive. A man that we detested united us in marriage. The affair smacked of racketeering. How can we be married right?" The fact is that nothing could be done. The one performing the service had reported the marriage. It was legal. No second license could be issued, and no annulment, if desired, was possible.

A young couple once came to me, who had been married by a "marrying parson." The manner in which they had been received by him and the way the service was performed was so disgusting to them, that they were not living together as man and wife. Some time was required before this disappointment could be overcome.

Even if you are not a church member, you want your wedding to be beautiful and meaningful. Clergymen are trained to solemnize marriages. They prepare for the occasion as they would for any sacred office of the church. The wedding certificate presented by a minister is attractive and beautiful; that received from a "marrying parson" or civil authority usually resembles a receipt for money paid. A clergyman can make the marriage ceremony beautiful.

Approximately three fourths of all the marriages in the United States are performed by clergymen, but these statistics do not exclude those at which "marrying parsons" officiate. A couple who is married by a minister in the community will have a friend from whom they can receive counsel in planning their wedding and making adjustments during the early years of their marital life. The minister keeps confidences and can be trusted with a knowledge of personal and intimate problems which one may want to discuss confidentially.

Civil services are, as a rule, void of beauty, undignified, businesslike and smack of the commercial. They form a legal tie but do not bestow a spiritual benediction. A prayer is usually omitted or read poorly and the service is performed in the name of the law, not in the Name of God. A divine institution is made a legal contract when a marriage is performed by someone other than a representative of the Church.

Your wedding should be shared with your family and your best friends. Make it an important and sacred occasion.

Research has revealed that when marriages are solemnized by clergymen, it is generally true that the couples are happier in marriage than those who were married by civil authorities. This can be explained perhaps by the fact that those who are married by a minister are eager to make their weddings more than mere legal contracts.

After the marriage, or wedding, the bridal party proceeds to the reception or dinner, then the couple leave alone for their honeymoon. They should be unaccompanied and go to a place where they are not well known.

The honeymoon affords an opportunity to realize their new status as man and wife. They should extend every courtesy and consideration to each other. There should be a mutual sharing of new experiences. Personal attractiveness should be maintained.

When the honeymoon is over the couple return to their apartment or home. It is better to live in one room than to live with parents or in-laws. A newly married couple should be left alone to develop their own marital standards. There should be no relatives or friends present to govern, suggest or supervise.

One of the joys of a bride's early married life is to arrange her own home, be it ever so simple. She should not be denied this privilege or be forced to postpone it unduly.

Every man is more natural in his own home even though it be humble. There is nothing that will strengthen and unify a marriage more than responsibility. Accept the obligation, at least, of paying rent for the place where you live. Such an investment will mean more to you than your savings.

When you are married you will want to safeguard your

marital happiness. To do this, follow the wisdom revealed by research and make yours a Christian home.

Suggested Reading for Further Study

I. COURTSHIP

Booth-Clibborn, Catherine. **Love and Courtship.** New York: Association Press.

Burkhart, Roy A. **From Friendship to Marriage.** New York: Harpers.

Murray, Alfred. **Youth's Courtship Problems.** Grand Rapids: Zondervan.

Strain, Frances B. **Love at the Threshold.** New York: Appleton-Century.

Wood, L. F. **Making A Home: A Study of Youth, Courtship and Marriage.** Nashville: Abingdon-Cokesbury.

II. PREPARATION FOR MARRIAGE

Blount, Ralph E. **Love Loyal.** Nashville: Abingdon-Cokesbury.

Dahlberg, Edwin. **Youth and the Homes of Tomorrow.** Philadelphia: Judson Press.

Folsom, Joseph K. **Plan for Marriage.** New York: Harpers.

Groves, Ernest R. **Preparation for Marriage.** New York: Emerson Books.

Nelson, Janet F., and Hiller, Margaret. **Marriages Are Not Made in Heaven.** New York: Woman's Press.

Popenoe, Paul. **Modern Marriage.** New York: Macmillan.

Van Keuren, Floyd. **Outfitting for Spiritual Marriage.** New York: Morehouse.

Wiley, Bell. **So You're Going to Get Married.** Philadelphia: Lippincott.

III. LOVE PROBLEMS

Butterfield, Oliver. **Love Problems of Adolescence.** New York: Emerson.

Dell, Floyd. **Love in a Machine Age.** New York: Farrar and Rinehart.

Galloway, T. W. **Love and Marriage.** New York: Funk and Wagnalls.

Murray, Alfred. **Youth's Problem No. 1.** Grand Rapids: Zondervan.

Reik, Theodore. **A Psychologist Looks At Love.** New York: Farrar and Rinehart.

IV. PERSONALITY DEVELOPMENT

Boorman, W. R. **Personality in Its Teens.** New York: Macmillan.
Groves, Ernest R. **Personality and Social Adjustment.** New York: Longmans.
Hart, Hornell, and Ella B. **Personality and the Family.** Boston: Heath.
Kern, Marjorie D. **Getting Along Together.** New York: McBride.
Mowrer, Harriet R. **Personality Adjustment and Domestic Discord.** New York: American Book Co.
Valentine, P. F. **The Psychology of Personality.** New York: Appleton.

V. ETIQUETTE

Allen, Betty, and Briggs, Mitchell P. **Behave Yourself!** Philadelphia: Lippincott.
Irwin, John. **Manners and Personality in School and Business.** Philadelphia: Winston.
Jonathan, Norton. **Gentlemen Aren't Sissies.** Philadelphia: Winston.
Post, Emily. **Etiquette.** New York: Funk and Wagnalls.
Vogue's Book of Brides. New York: Doubleday Doran.

VI. SEX EDUCATION

Arden, Theodore, and Dickinson, Robert. **A Handbook for Husbands and Wives.** New York: Association Press.
Billy, Ceyril. **Sex Education.** New York, Emerson.
Butterfield, Oliver. **Marriage and Sexual Harmony.** New York: Emerson Books.
Davis, Katherine. **Sex Factors in the Lives of 2,200 Women.** New York: Harpers.
Groves, Ernest R., Gladys H., and Catherine. **Sex Fulfillment in Marriage.** New York: Emerson Books.
Stone, Hannah, and Abraham. **A Marriage Manual.** New York: Simon and Schuster.

VII. MARITAL HAPPINESS

Binkley, Robert, and Frances. **What Is Right with Marriage?** New York: Appleton-Century.
Burgess, E. W., and Cottrell, Leonard S. **Predicting Success or Failure in Marriage.** New York: Prentice-Hall.
Dickinson, R. L., and Beam, Laura. **One Thousand Marriages.** Baltimore: Williams and Wilkins.
Hamilton, G. V. **A Research in Marriage.** New York: Boni and Liveright.
Hamilton, G. V., and Macgowan, Kenneth. **What's Wrong with Marriage?** New York: Boni and Liveright.

Hart, Hornell. **Chart for Happiness.** New York: Macmillan.
Sanger, Margaret. **Happiness in Marriage.** New York: Blue Ribbon Books.
Terman, Lewis M. **Psychological Factors in Marital Happiness.** New York: McGraw-Hill.

VIII. MARRIAGE (General)

Baber, Ray E. **Marriage and the Family.** New York: McGraw-Hill.
Bowman. Henry A. **Marriage for Moderns.** New York: McGraw-Hill.
Duvall, Evelyn M., and Hill, Reuben. **When You Marry.** New York: Association.
Foster, Robert G. **Marriage and Family Relationships.** New York: Macmillan.
Groves, Ernest R. **Marriage.** New York: Henry Holt and Co.
Himes, Norman E. **Your Marriage.** New York: Farrar and Rinehart.
Jung, Moses. **Modern Marriage.** New York: F. S. Crofts Co.
Keyserling, Herman. **The Book of Marriage.** New York: Harcourt, Brace, and Co.
Nash, A. S. **Education for Christian Marriage.** New York: Macmillan.
Popenoe, Paul. **Marriage Before and After.** New York: Wilfred Funk.

Sex Problems of the Returned Veteran, by Howard Kitching, M.D., published by Emerson Books Inc., 251 West 15th Street, New York ($1.50), is a recent book that will prove invaluable to the returned veteran and his wife in successfully rebuilding their marriage after the emotional upheaval of war.

How to Pick a Mate, by Clifford R. Adams, published by E. P. Dutton and Company. New York City ($2.75), is a readable and timely volume offering guidance to those seeking a happy marriage. A wide reading of this book should help to decrease the high divorce rate.

Printed in the United States of America.